Idaho

A Bicentennial History

F. Ross Peterson

W. W. Norton & Company, Inc.
New York

American Association for State and Local History
Nashville

Published and distributed by
W. W. Norton & Co., Inc.
500 Fifth Avenue
New York, New York 10036

Library of Congress Cataloguing-in-Publication Data

Peterson, Frank Ross.
Idaho, a bicentennial history.

(The States and the Nation series)
Bibliography: p.
Includes index.
1. Idaho—History. I. Title. II. Series.
F746.P47   979.6   76–26873
ISBN 0–393–05600–7
Printed in the United States of America
2 3 4 5 6 7 8 9 0

To Mother and Dad
who were and are Idaho

Contents

Illustrations

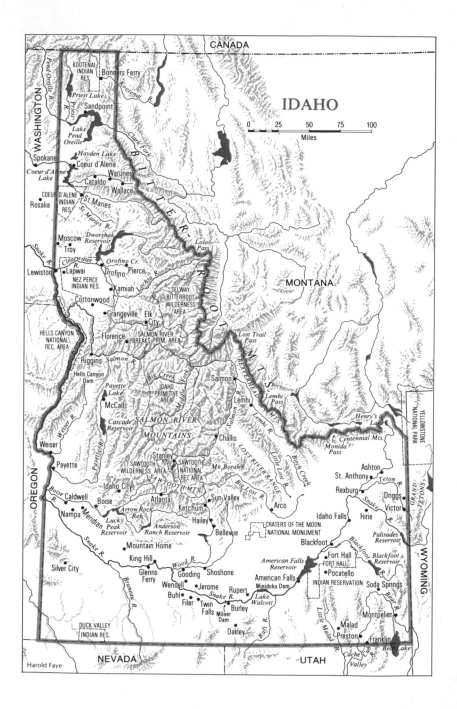

CANADA

IDAHO

0   25   50   75   100
Miles

WASHINGTON

KOOTENAI INDIAN RES.
Bonners Ferry

Pend Oreille R.
Priest Lake
Priest R.
Kootenai R.
Sandpoint

Lake Pend Oreille

Clark Fork

Spokane
Hayden Lake
Coeur d'Alene
Coeur d'Alene Lake
Wardner
Cataldo
Wallace

Rosalia
COEUR D'ALENE INDIAN RES.
St. Maries
St. Maries R.

Snake R.
Moscow
Dworshak Reservoir
Troy
Clearwater R.
Lewiston
Lapwai
NEZ PERCE INDIAN RES.
Orofino Cr.
Orofino
Pierce
Kamiah
Cottonwood
Lochsa R.
Lolo Pass
SELWAY-BITTERROOT WILDERNESS AREA

Grangeville
Elk City

HELLS CANYON NATIONAL REC. AREA
Florence
SALMON RIVER BREAKS PRIM. AREA
Lost Trail Pass

Riggins
Salmon R.

Hells Canyon Dam
Big Creek
IDAHO PRIMITIVE AREA
Middle Fork Salmon R.
Salmon
Lemhi
Lemhi Pass

MONTANA

BITTER-ROOT MTS.

BEAVERHEAD MTS.

Lemhi R.
Lemhi MTS.

Payette Lake
McCall

Weiser R.
Cascade Reservoir
SALMON RIVER MOUNTAINS
Challis
Salmon R.
LOST RIVER RANGE
Birch Creek
Henry's Lake
Centennial Mts.
Monida Pass

YELLOWSTONE NATIONAL PARK

Weiser

Payette

Caldwell
Boise R.
Nampa
Meridian
Boise

Idaho City
SAWTOOTH WILDERNESS AREA
Stanley
SAWTOOTH NATIONAL REC. AREA
SAWTOOTH MTS.
Mt. Borah
Big Lost R.
Sun Valley
Arco

Ashton
St. Anthony
Teton R.
Rexburg
Driggs
Victor
Snake R.
Ririe

Payette R.
Atlanta
Ketchum
Little Lost R.

OREGON

Silver City

Arrow Rock Res.
Lucky Peak Reservoir
Anderson Ranch Reservoir
Hailey
Bellevue
CRATERS OF THE MOON NATIONAL MONUMENT

Idaho Falls

Palisades Reservoir

GRAND TETONS

WYOMING

Snake R.
Mountain Home
King Hill
Wood R.
Glenns Ferry
Gooding
Shoshone

American Falls Reservoir
American Falls
Minidoka Dam
Blackfoot
Fort Hall
FORT HALL INDIAN RESERVATION
Pocatello
Blackfoot R.
Blackfoot Reservoir
Soda Springs
Bear R.

Bruneau R.
Wendell
Jerome
Rupert
Snake R.
Buhl
Filer
Twin Falls
Milner Dam
Burley
Lake Walcott

DUCK VALLEY INDIAN RES.

Raft R.
Oakley

Little Malad R.
Malad
Preston
Montpelier
Franklin
Bear Lake
Cache Valley
Cache R.

NEVADA
UTAH

Harold Faye

Invitation to the Reader

IN 1807, former President John Adams argued that a complete history of the American Revolution could not be written until the history of change in each state was known, because the principles of the Revolution were as various as the states that went through it. Two hundred years after the Declaration of Independence, the American nation has spread over a continent and beyond. The states have grown in number from thirteen to fifty. And democratic principles have been interpreted differently in every one of them.

We therefore invite you to consider that the history of your state may have more to do with the bicentennial review of the American Revolution than does the story of Bunker Hill or Valley Forge. The Revolution has continued as Americans extended liberty and democracy over a vast territory. John Adams was right: the states are part of that story, and the story is incomplete without an account of their diversity.

The Declaration of Independence stressed life, liberty, and the pursuit of happiness; accordingly, it shattered the notion of holding new territories in the subordinate status of colonies. The Northwest Ordinance of 1787 set forth a procedure for new states to enter the Union on an equal footing with the old. The Federal Constitution shortly confirmed this novel means of building a nation out of equal states. The step-by-step process through which territories have achieved self-government and national representation is among the most important of the Founding Fathers' legacies.

The method of state-making reconciled the ancient conflict between liberty and empire, resulting in what Thomas Jefferson called an empire for liberty. The system has worked and remains unaltered, despite enormous changes that have taken

place in the nation. The country's extent and variety now surpass anything the patriots of '76 could likely have imagined.
The United States has changed from an agrarian republic into a
highly industrial and urban democracy, from a fledgling nation
into a major world power. As Oliver Wendell Holmes remarked
in 1920, the creators of the nation could not have seen completely how it and its constitution and its states would develop.
Any meaningful review in the bicentennial era must consider
what the country has become, as well as what it was.

The new nation of equal states took as its motto *E Pluribus
Unum*—"out of many, one." But just as many peoples have
become Americans without complete loss of ethnic and cultural
identities, so have the states retained differences of character.
Some have been superficial, expressed in stereotyped images—
big, boastful Texas, "sophisticated" New York, "hillbilly"
Arkansas. Other differences have been more real, sometimes instructively, sometimes amusingly; democracy has embraced
Huey Long's Louisiana, bilingual New Mexico, unicameral Nebraska, and a Texas that once taxed fortunetellers and spawned
politicians called "Woodpecker Republicans" and "Skunk
Democrats." Some differences have been profound, as when
South Carolina secessionists led other states out of the Union in
opposition to abolitionists in Massachusetts and Ohio. The result was a bitter Civil War.

The Revolution's first shots may have sounded in Lexington
and Concord; but fights over what democracy should mean and
who should have independence have erupted from Pennsylvania's Gettysburg to the "Bleeding Kansas" of John Brown,
from the Alamo in Texas to the Indian battles at Montana's
Little Bighorn. Utah Mormons have known the strain of isolation; Hawaiians at Pearl Harbor, the terror of attack; Georgians
during Sherman's march, the sadness of defeat and devastation.
Each state's experience differs instructively; each adds under-
standing to the whole.

The purpose of this series of books is to make that kind of un-
derstanding accessible, in a way that will last in value far
beyond the bicentennial fireworks. The series offers a volume
on every state, plus the District of Columbia—fifty-one, in all.

Each book contains, besides the text, a view of the state through eyes other than the author's—a "photographer's essay," in which a skilled photographer presents his own personal perceptions of the state's contemporary flavor.

We have asked authors not for comprehensive chronicles, nor for research monographs or new data for scholars. Bibliographies and footnotes are minimal. We have asked each author for a summing up—interpretive, sensitive, thoughtful, individual, even personal—of what seems significant about his or her state's history. What distinguishes it? What has mattered about it, to its own people and to the rest of the nation? What has it come to now?

To interpret the states in all their variety, we have sought a variety of backgrounds in authors themselves and have encouraged variety in the approaches they take. They have in common only these things: historical knowledge, writing skill, and strong personal feelings about a particular state. Each has wide latitude for the use of the short space. And if each succeeds, it will be by offering you, in your capacity as a *citizen* of a state *and* of a nation, stimulating insights to test against your own.

James Morton Smith
General Editor

Idaho

1

Idaho: Nature's Gift
to Man

IDAHO did not begin with Lewis, Clark, or Sacajawea. Nor did it begin when the first native Americans
crossed rivers, mountains, or invisible lines into what is
now Idaho. Both the Indians and the white explorers appreciated
and respected the land that became Idaho; yet the land ante-
dates their arrival. In reality, Idaho's beginning is the evolving
artistic achievements of nature as the waters splashed, the winds
carved, and the volcanoes erupted. The result is a magnificent region of mountains, rivers, canyons, lakes, and painted
deserts.

The name *Idaho* induces an unusual state of mind. Fourth-
and seventh-grade students are often taught that Idaho means
"gem of the mountains." Scholars know that *Idaho* is not an
Indian word and probably has no Indian derivation. It was proposed as a name for Colorado, and, since it lost there, Congress
attached the name to one of the next areas that applied for territorial status. Yet, the word does mean something now—it con-
jures up visions of openness and vastness, with continually re-
curring manifestations of nature's versatility.

Contemporary observers may travel the state from north to
south or east to west, and their impressions will be as divergent
as the picturesque scenery. Chances are they will not remember

much about the five or six small Idaho cities. Instead they will
remember that a sunset on the Grand Tetons, viewed from the
western Teton Valley, is an unparalleled experience. Or the observer might travel down U. S. Highway 12, close to where
Lewis and Clark actually rode on the Lolo Trail, and for nearly
a hundred miles see only forests, mountains, water, and animals. Or it might be the tumbling water as it cascades over the
jagged rocks at Shoshone, Twin, or Idaho Falls of the Snake
River, or the splendor of the spectacular Moyie Falls in the narrow northern Panhandle that enchants the viewer. Some might
even be so lucky as to catch a world-record trout from the deep
blue waters of Priest Lake or spend a day mystified by the rich
turquoise color of Bear Lake, finding it difficult to realize that
those two lakes are separated by over five hundred miles of
mountains, forests, and deserts.

A few daring and adventuresome souls may don backpacks
and climb into the primitive areas hoping for a glimpse of wild
sheep or elk or moose or a view of the endless sea of mountains. Others may enjoy the thrill of seeing a bear trudge along a
rural road near Bonners Ferry. The barren desolation of the lava
beds in and near Craters of the Moon National Monument is
always impressive as a stark reminder of nature's power.
Modern-day travelers interested in the developments of a tech-
nological age will appreciate Idaho's dams, canals, and electric
sprinkler systems that provide water for a thirsty soil to produce
crops—especially potatoes—in rich abundance. On the other
hand, some might be concerned and even depressed by the vi-
sual evidences of man's continual exploitation of Idaho's great
mineral wealth—the slag piles and strip mines.

Idaho is a state full of natural phenomena and cultural diversification. In many ways its ironies and confusions are those
shared by the entire nation. Politically, Idaho has a populist-
progressive tradition, yet it usually votes conservatively. It has
always been the Pacific Northwest's geographic tie to the northern plains and the Great Basin. Lewis and Clark, the Astorians,
the British and American fur trappers, Bonneville and Frémont,
and the Oregon-bound pioneers viewed Idaho as a crossroads. It
was a place to get through, not one in which to sink roots.

Consequently, the state has remained a fairly isolated and sparsely populated hinterland. This will not always be the case. Idaho's vast water resources attract the eye of a thirsty and dry California, and her minerals and timber are being coveted by an energy-conscious nation. The conservation versus exploitation battles will be fought, and Idaho may well be a major area of confrontation.

Much can be gleaned from the experience of this semi-isolated mountain wilderness state and its contribution to the history of the nation. Idaho has had a dynamic past filled with diversity, irony, and conflict; Idaho possesses much that is important to the nation's future. It is here that the American citizenry may find the potential to conserve and preserve and restore. This is Idaho's opportunity and its challenge to the nation that granted it statehood in 1890.

When Congress during the Civil War completed its geographical carving in the northern Rocky Mountains, it had no idea what it had done. From the old Oregon Country and the territory of Washington, it created the territory of Idaho, originally larger than Texas. After organizing and naming the territory in 1863, Congress chopped away at the eastern boundary until by 1868, Wyoming and Montana were separate identities. What remained was a geographical entity whose boundaries resembled a side view of a rustic, hand-carved church pew or, as one humorist called it, "a pregnant capital L." John Corlett of Boise called it a crazy patchwork of a state and postulated that geographically Idaho is a state that should not have been. Bordered by six other states and British Columbia, Idaho's unique geographical boundaries are another ramification of diversity.

The southern boundary is over three hundred miles long and follows the 42nd parallel, the line which separated American and English claims from the Spanish claims to the Rockies. Idaho's Canadian boundary on the north is approximately forty-five miles across. Since the Oregon boundary was established by 1863, the southwestern border of Idaho was already determined. Over two hundred miles of the nearly five-hundred-mile western boundary are formed by the Snake River and its Hells Canyon. After crossing the entire state of Idaho from east to west, the Snake River veers northward. At that point, the mapmakers drew a line straight south, slightly west of the 117th meridian, to intersect the 42nd parallel and form the southwestern corner of the state. The Snake travels northward for approximately two hundred miles and then moves westward toward a union with the Columbia. Where the Snake begins its westward course through Washington, a line two miles west of the 117th meridian was drawn north to Canada. Although there are international and natural boundaries to help explain the creation of the northern, southern, and western borders, the eastern boundary is confusing and almost inexplicable. At one time, it was proposed that the eastern border be the continental divide all the way from the 42nd parallel to Canada. What exists now is an eight-hundred-mile line that begins with an extension of the Utah border northward three miles east of the 111th meridian to the continental divide inside Yellowstone National Park. Then the boundary follows the continental divide westward for approximately two hundred miles. Near Lost Trail Pass, the artificial line leaves the divide and moves northwest along the crest of the majestic Bitterroot Mountains. Nearly one hundred miles from the Canadian border, the line is drawn straight north just west of the 116th meridian. This narrow northernmost section sandwiched between Washington and Montana is the Panhandle.

Inside these artificial and natural borders are 83,557 square miles of land and nearly eight hundred thousand people. With approximately nine individuals per square mile, Idaho is still sparsely populated. It ranks thirteenth among the states in land size but is forty-second in population. This is now the state of Idaho—a rough mountainous and arid desert triangular land mass. Nature and law are responsible for one of the most fascinating, yet incongruent of states. Indeed, the mountains, water, minerals, timber, and wildlife of Idaho give the state as great an identity as that of its people.

Water—and its controlled agricultural usage—was essential to the development of Idaho. Few natural resources are guarded as selfishly by Idahoans as is their water. Numerous great river systems cross Idaho, and two large rivers are contained entirely within the state's boundaries. With the eastern border on the continental divide and the western border dropping to 735 feet above sea level, there is a tremendous flow of surface water. The many streams carry enough water for hydroelectric power, industry, urban needs, and irrigation, yet still provide for the needs of native fish and game. In a day when wells are replacing canals, the large accompanying underground aquifer is being tapped for multiple use as well.

Perhaps the single most unifying geographical feature of Idaho is the roaring Snake River. Referred to as the River of the Sagebrush Plain by the Shoshoni Indians, the river has its source in the mountains of Yellowstone National Park. From the southern part of Yellowstone, it flows through the trapper's paradise of Jackson Hole and then west into Idaho. The river follows an inverted arc across the state to Oregon and then turns north through Hells Canyon—Idaho is on its right and Oregon and Washington are on its left. At Lewiston it joins the Clearwater and swings west for 140 miles toward a confluence with the mighty Columbia River. In length, volume of water carried, and area drained, the Snake ranks sixth among the rivers of America. In more specific terms, it is 1,036 miles long and drains 109,000 square miles of country, an area larger than the entire state of Idaho. This gigantic stream drains the mountain runoff from all of Idaho except the Bear River valley in the southeastern corner of the state and the lake-dominated Panhandle. By the time the Snake reaches the Columbia it has increased its volume from four to forty million acre feet of water and has dropped more than seven thousand feet in elevation.

The Snake River was never viewed as a friendly stream by westward-moving pioneers. It was difficult to cross and the canyons in many areas are so deep that the water was always near, yet inaccessible. The Snake flows through mountain gorges and lava beds and has a number of sizable waterfalls, including the spectacular Shoshone Falls, which at 212 feet is higher than Niagara. The appropriately named Hells Canyon of the Snake River cuts a gorge deeper than any other in the United States. In some places it reaches a depth of 7,900 feet and is also one of the narrowest canyons on the continent. In many parts of the canyon are green forests, but at other points are sheer walls splashed by the seasonal color of mountain shrubbery. When the Oregon-bound pioneers viewed this impassable canyon, they left the Snake and headed west across Oregon's Blue Mountains toward the coveted Willamette Valley.

To the extent that Idaho is tied together, it is the Snake River and its valley that provide a cord of cohesion. The five major Idaho cities are located on the Snake or its tributaries, and this one river system provides the irrigation water and hydroelectric power to ensure agricultural prosperity, domestic water supplies, and a degree of industrialization. Without the harnessing of the water of the Snake, Idaho would still be a mountain and desert wilderness. The major tributaries of the Snake contribute to the role of that river as the unifying geographical feature in Idaho.

The most dramatic and romantic of Idaho's rivers is the wild and rugged "River of No Return," the Salmon. A spawning stream for the powerful salmon, it seems that only the salmon and jet-powered boats can navigate the stream upriver, and only expert guides attempt to descend. For 425 miles the Salmon and its numerous raging tributaries wind their way through the spectacular mountains of central Idaho. Like the Snake, the Salmon has several distinctive characteristics. It is one of the longest American streams lying wholly within one state, and its canyon gorge is deeper than that of the Grand Canyon of the Colorado River. It flows from the Sawtooth Wilderness Area through four national forests, and its drainage includes the famous Idaho Primitive Area. After flowing all four major directions, it joins the Snake about fifty miles south of Lewiston. Still basically a wild and unmolested river, the Salmon has not yet been invaded by human technology and energy-producing projects. Consequently, the river has not been harnessed for agricultural or hydroelectric purposes.

Another major river system lying wholly within the state is the Clearwater of northern Idaho. The Bitterroot Mountains on the Idaho-Montana border provide the headwaters for the streams that become the Clearwater. This river felt the impact of man to a great degree and much earlier than other Idaho streams. The Clearwater system carried the Lewis and Clark expedition to the Snake and was used also for the return voyage. Gold was first discovered in Idaho on a tributary of the Clearwater, this system thus becoming the site of the original Idaho gold rush. The surrounding mountains are covered by dense stands of white pine and Douglas fir, and the Clearwater was the scene of one of the last genuine river log drives in the United States.

A particularly peculiar river, the meandering Bear, passes through a corner of Idaho. This relatively small stream is exceptional because it is approximately three hundred miles long and does not flow to an ocean. Its source is in Utah's high Uinta Mountains. Moving northward, on a trek reminiscent of a serpent's path, it winds back and forth undecidedly from Utah to Wyoming to Utah to Wyoming before it finally enters Idaho. After moving north toward the tributaries of the Snake, it veers to the southwest, eventually returning to Utah and depositing its water into the Great Salt Lake. Early trappers found beaver treasures along the Bear, and the Oregon Trail entered Idaho with the Bear and followed it for a considerable distance. For many whites, the Bear River valley provided their first glimpse of what was to become Idaho. Although the river has contributed to some economic and agricultural development of the state, it is also one of the many forces that tie southeastern Idaho to Utah.

There are many powerful rivers in the north, but, like the Bear, their impact is not so significant or Idaho-oriented as the Snake and its tributaries. The Kootenai and Pend Oreille flow toward the north and eventually merge directly with the Columbia. A dynamic river, the Clark Fork, is the largest source of water for beautiful Lake Pend Oreille. The Pend Oreille River flows out of the lake toward a juncture with the Columbia near the Canada-Washington border. Three historic rivers, Saint Maries, Saint Joe, and the Coeur d'Alene, flow into Coeur d'Alene Lake. They abounded with fish and later provided the natural waterway for bringing timber to market. The Spokane River carries the waters of Coeur d'Alene Lake across eastern Washington to the Columbia. Although there are numerous smaller streams that contribute to Idaho's water resources, they are the tributaries that become the great rivers. The Boise, Payette, and various forks of the Salmon add magnificently to the scenic splendor of the state.

Idaho diverts an enormous amount of water from its source. The Snake is dammed eleven times in Idaho alone, and most of its tributaries contain at least one major reservoir. The Boise River system has five dams, and several others have nearly as many. It is the diverted water that furnished the means of agrarian survival for the whites who remained in the Snake River valley.

Agricultural products are the state's greatest source of wealth and attest to the success of irrigation as a means to create productivity. The Snake River and its statewide valley system are where most of Idaho's farmers reside and seek prosperity. Although Idaho potatoes have received considerable fame and publicity and a spot on license plates, Idaho has other noteworthy crops. Sugar beets, peas, and beans are grown throughout the southern part of the state as well as in the Panhandle. Grains such as wheat, barley, corn, and oats all survive Idaho's arid climate. Of course, the beef, dairy, and sheep industries operate throughout the state, but are especially strong along the Snake River. In fact, beef and sheep utilize the vast public lands of Idaho for controlled grazing during the summer months. In the Snake River valley northwest of Boise and near Lewiston are numerous fruit orchards.

If it were not for Idaho's numerous rivers and the countless irrigation systems, below and above the surface, most southern Idaho farmers could not survive the arid climate with its minimal valley precipitation. Lack of rainfall is one reason the pioneers seeking cheap land were reluctant to stop to try their fortunes in Idaho. Control of the spring runoff from the melting mountain snows became the key to tilling the soil. Water was, and is still, the key to the state's development.

Although the powerful rivers provide the lifeblood to Idaho, the mountain lakes and reservoirs provide aesthetic beauty and recreation beyond compare. It is the mountain setting that distinguishes these varied bodies of water. There are in excess of

two thousand charted lakes, most of which are found in high alpine valleys. The larger and most noted of the Idaho lakes are
found either upon elevated plateaus or at the bases of the loftier
mountains in the Panhandle. The surrounding terrain varies
from forests reaching the shoreline to more open grassland and
thickets. All of these lakes offer great recreational as well as
scenic appeal.

In the far northwest corner of Idaho lies Priest Lake. Semisur-
rounded by the Kaniksu National Forest, this lake has always
provided ideal fishing and was heavily used by early trappers.
About twenty miles southeast of Priest Lake is the largest lake
in the state, Lake Pend Oreille, whose surface area covers 180
square miles. A navy base, Farragut, built on the western shore
during World War II, has since become a mammoth state park.
One of the earliest white visitors to the area, David Thompson,
built a trading post, Kullyspell House, at Pend Oreille. A few
miles to the south of Lake Pend Oreille are two other lakes
which have become diversions and the playthings of Spokane,
Washington, residents. Hayden Lake is almost completely surrounded by summer homes; yet, its forested setting creates an
illusion of isolation. Coeur d'Alene Lake is one of the most
popular resort areas in Idaho and provides unexcelled water recreation. All of these Panhandle lakes benefit from their proximity to national forests. The evergreens stop where the deep blue
waters begin, and the contrasting blue water and green foliage
against an azure sky are guarantees of delightful scenery.

Heavily timbered and sparsely populated central Idaho also
possesses a number of high mountain lakes of note. The Payette
Lakes near McCall are outstanding for their beauty. This region
gets more snow than any other inhabited section of Idaho, and
the resulting late spring prevents recreational use of these lakes
from destroying the ecology. Although two hours north of
Boise, many citizens of the state's capital find relaxation in the
Payette Lakes. Other more adventuresome outdoor people will
go into the Sawtooth National Recreation Area northeast of
Boise to the high mountain Redfish, Stanley, or Alturas lakes.
With fewer people and more fish, these lakes provide a remote
paradise.

Eastern Idaho depends on reservoirs for its recreation except for two notable exceptions. In the northeastern corner of the state, only fifteen miles from Yellowstone, is the small but historic Henry's Lake. A fantastic fishing lake, where the trout mature rapidly, it was a significant landmark for the earliest American fur trappers when they crossed into Idaho. Another favorite trapper rendezvous was at Bear Lake in the far southeastern corner of the state. Half of this lake is in Utah. Depending on the time of day, year, and the texture of the sky, this remarkably deep lake demonstrates colors beyond compare. The water reflects so many shades of blue that it is baffling. Perhaps most unforgettable are the days that the lake becomes turquoise. There are thousands of high mountain lakes in Idaho, and it is probably best that most go unmentioned because even though Idahoans are proud of their natural beauties, there are special little-known areas that still maintain a desirable loneliness.

As much as natural lakes provide recreational and aesthetic appreciation, manmade reservoirs are also important to Idaho's past, present, and future. Many of these bodies of water rival the lakes in beauty and appeal. The Snake River and its tributaries have been dammed so many times that numerous large reservoirs exist. The dams, although constructed for hydroelectric or irrigation purposes, are significant additions to the Idaho waterscape.

The Palisades Lake on the Snake River, near the Wyoming line, is a heavily used recreational lake, and its setting rivals many of the natural lakes. The largest controlled body of water in Idaho is also on the Snake at American Falls. The Blackfoot, Anderson Ranch, Lucky Peak, Cascade, and the Dworshak dam reservoirs are all heavily used for recreation and fishing. Combined, the thousands of lakes and reservoirs give Idaho not only a vast recreational facility but also document once again that water is the blood that flows through the veins of Idaho and sustains human, animal, and plant life.

Idaho's mountainous terrain provides one explanation for the abundance of water. The average elevation of Idaho is over five thousand feet above sea level. Only four states are higher. Although the river valleys provide an agrarian foothold for human beings, the numerous mountain ranges offer another aspect to Idaho. Wildlife and minerals are found throughout the mountains, and those two resources led to white discovery, exploration, and organization of the area. And those two resources continue to cause ecological debates throughout the state. Add the development of recreation facilities to hunting and prospecting, and it becomes apparent that Idaho's mountains, alpine valleys, and primitive areas face a new wave of human invasion.

Nearly 40 percent of the area of the entire state is national forest land. Central Idaho is continuous mountains that have yet to feel the full imprint of four-wheel-drive vehicles. The Sawtooth Mountains are distinct for beautiful high granite crags, wooded slopes, and well-watered miniature valleys and meadows. The White Cloud Peaks, Boulder Mountains, and Sawtooth Range all have many peaks above the ten-thousand-foot level, and these mountains are the habitat of numerous big game animals.

The loftiest range of Idaho mountains is the unique and mysterious Lost River Range. The range runs in a northwestern-southeastern direction for eighty miles through central Idaho. On each side of the range is a long narrow valley with a sizable stream of water. In both cases, the Big and Little Lost rivers sink into the lava beds southeast of the mountain range. The entire crest of the Lost River Range is in excess of 10,000 feet, except for a few passes. Idaho's three highest peaks, all over 12,000 feet, are found in this range, including Mount Borah, which at 12,662 feet is the highest point in Idaho. With a skyline so majestic and with the thick green forests in contrast to the snowcapped peaks, the Lost River Range is a grand world of its own.

All along the Idaho-Montana border there is a natural boundary of mountain ranges. Much of the border proximates the continental divide, and the Centennial and the Beaverhead mountains in northeastern Idaho are deceptive in their magnitude. It was these mountains that trappers first crossed in entering Idaho. The Bitterroot Mountains begin where the Beaverhead Range ends, and the Bitterroots extend nearly to Lake Pend Oreille. With the deep canyons, snowy ridges, and summits of nearly ten thousand feet, these mountains were originally deemed impassable by Lewis and Clark. Finally, the explorers discovered Lolo Pass and made their way to the Snake River system. This range is almost meadowless and features numerous sharp crags and white granite. The primitive area contained in the Bitterroots is filled with bighorns, mountain goats, elk, bear, and other wildlife.

The largest group of mountains in Idaho lies in the Clearwaters of northern Idaho. Although fascinating and well watered, these mountains rarely exceed 8,000 feet. This area is one of heavy logging, and the mountain foliage reflects this human presence. Second to the Clearwater range are the mountains of the Salmon River Range. Found in central Idaho north of the Sawtooths, these mountains contain the huge Idaho Primitive Area and the spectacularly rugged Bighorn Crags. Roads are scarce into the rough bare granite crags, yet aerial photography and adventuresome backpackers attest that the Bighorn Crags is one of the most rugged ranges of the entire Northwest.

A discussion of favorite Idaho mountain ranges could be endless. One authority numbered eighty-one separately named Idaho ranges. Numerous peaks exceed the ten-thousand-foot level. Not only do these mountains provide scenic wilderness retreats, rarely touched primitive areas, and recreational paradises, but they are also constantly involved in an ongoing industry-environmentalist debate concerning usage. Mineral deposits and lumber stands are the catalysts that involve the silent majestic mountains in unsought notoriety.

It was gold that ultimately brought territorial status to Idaho, and the mining industry has played an important part in the economic development of the state. Yet mineral resources and their exploitation have never brought statewide wealth. They have brought considerable labor strife and some ecological destruction.

Idaho is the nation's leading silver-producing state and Shoshone County in the Panhandle is the source for most of the silver. Many of the mines have been producing for nearly a century, and although millions of dollars worth of silver have been

produced, the tragic mine disasters and the ecological devastation have created mixed emotions in its citizens. In part, because of the type of ore found in northern Idaho, lead-silver or
lead-silver-zinc ore is mined in the same operations. Idaho is the
second leading lead producer in the nation. If it were not for the
use of lead by the battery and automobile industries, Idaho
profit would be considerably less. The silver-lead-zinc operations will continue to bring some prosperity to northern Idaho.

Southeastern Idaho extracts considerable wealth from the
mountains in the form of phosphate rock and its by-products, elemental phosphorous and vanadium. This industry has boomed
since World War II, the material being used mainly for the
production of agricultural fertilizers. Idaho ranks second to
Florida in phosphate production, yet seemingly has unending reserves. In the phosphate trade-off between man and the mountains, however, the mountains are the sorry losers. Much of the
mining has been of the strip variety, and the small ranges of
southeastern Idaho, south and east of Pocatello, have felt the
wrath of the bulldozer and "carryall." Severe air pollution has
been a constant problem with the processing plants, and, in
some cases, the effect of pollution on adjacent properties has
been disastrous. In 1970, Idaho ranked thirty-sixth nationally in
wealth provided by minerals, and it seems that that ranking will
not change drastically. Periodically, mining engineers and modern prospectors seek to exploit the wild and primitive mountains
of central Idaho. As more Idahoans redefine progress in non-
economic terms, it is likely that any new exploitation will ad-
here to strict environmentalist standards—a welcome development in preserving Idaho's heritage.

If for no other reason than that trees can be replaced, the
timber industry will probably continue to fare much better than
mining. Idaho was fortunate in that massive exploitation of
timber did not take place in the state until there had developed a
national conservation conscience. Of course, the mountains
have aided in the preservation of a timber supply. In the East,
South, and Midwest, timber was cleared in order to till the land.
That has rarely been the case in Idaho. Most of the virgin stands

are located in areas that make agriculture very unlikely. Currently, only four states produce more sawtimber than does Idaho.

From almost the beginning, multiple use has been the key management practice in Idaho's vast forests. Created during the Progressive period, Idaho was forced to think in terms of conservation and reforestation very early. While the Idaho timber industry is concerned chiefly with harvesting timber and simultaneously perpetuating the supply, it has had to co-operate with wildlife, recreation, and mining interests. Consequently, Idaho's wealth of green gold continues to provide the number one source of manufacturing income, and forest products are second only to agriculture in the entire state. And some timber industry spokesmen would lead the populace to believe that lumbering is farming. However, most of the timber is harvested from public lands.

Most of the excess of one hundred billion board feet of lumber cut in Idaho is the evergreen or conifer classification. Less than 1 percent are broadleaf hardwoods. The Douglas fir is the state's greatest producer, with the other pines and firs following way behind. The towering Western white pine is the state's declared tree, and it is found mostly north of the Clearwater. Some white pines have grown to heights of around two hundred feet. Currently there are thirteen national forests headquartered in Idaho, and they represent a monument to federal, state, and private co-operation. Combined with the federally dedicated wilderness areas of more than three million acres, Idaho's forests, mountains, and streams offer a legitimate return to nature.

Over twenty million acres of Idaho's forests are controlled by the national government. In fact, 63.7 percent of Idaho land is federally owned. Only three other states—Alaska, Utah, and Nevada—have a higher percentage of federal ownership. Alaska is the only state that has more national forest acreage. Since these forests are part of the federal reserve, their utilization and exploitation will depend on the needs, wishes, and desires of the federal government.

At times, contemporary Idahoans are irritated when they realize that Idaho is an economic colony of the federal government, with less than 40 percent of Idaho's land in private hands. Most of the nearly thirty-four million acres of federal property is national forest, but there are millions of acres controlled by the Bureau of Land Management, the Atomic Energy Commission, and the Bureau of Indian Affairs. When the federal bureaucracies overlap, the frustration leads to futility and anger.

When Idaho's fabulous mountain wonderland is contemplated, it is interesting to note that no national parks are headquartered within the state. A thin strip of Yellowstone is included in Idaho, but its impact is insignificant. Idaho's national legislators have followed a different track that is unique. Rather than bend to the tourist promotion industry, they have not pushed for national park status that would have led to hordes of humans clad in the garb of tourism. Instead, they have created one national recreation area in the Sawtooth Mountains east of Stanley and another in the lower Hells Canyon south of Lewiston. Legislators have sought wilderness or primitive status for other areas of the central Idaho mountains. In bureaucratic definition, this means that these areas are to be preserved as they exist.

There is one national monument within the state, the Craters of the Moon. Situated in the south central part of Idaho, these lava beds have a distinct resemblance to a moonscape. With the numerous caves and craters, this weird and impressive monument is the scene of volcanic activity. Interestingly, this barren area is only a few short miles from some of Idaho's highest and most beautiful mountain valleys. The National Park Service has recommended the creation of two more national monuments in Idaho: City of Rocks on the California Trail, and the Hagerman fossils along the Snake River.

What federal ownership of Idaho's mountains often means is that the state is economically dependent upon Washington, D.C. As it stands now, Idaho's citizens appear to be willing to avoid the temptation of selling their powerful and magnificent natural heritage for a mess of temporary prosperity. If an industry-oriented federal government finds a compatible philosophy in Idaho's state government, preservation and conservation may lose out to the drive for exploitation.

It is well to mention Idaho's other resource. Although water, agriculture, mining, and timber are of significance, so are Idaho's people. The bulging L-shaped state is largely uninhabited, and because of geography, Idaho is only now developing a statewide identity. Although the state is eighty-five years old, it has taken that long to pull the state together. If Idaho had no right to exist geographically, it has had to develop other common traits and ideals. Idaho's human story is how the people came to be Idahoans.

Idaho has looked three different directions for economic prosperity, media contact, and cultural compatibility. There have been at least three Idahos: one in the Panhandle, one in the southeastern part of the state, and one in the southwest around Boise. The Panhandle is geographically isolated from the remainder of the state and always has been since territorial days. With their mining and lumber orientation, the people have looked to Spokane as the center of their world. Their commerce passed through Spokane, and at various times they have discussed the formation of a new state.

Southeastern Idaho was almost completely settled by Mormon pioneers moving north from Utah. The area from the Wyoming border westward to the Idaho Falls area and south to the Utah line is an extension of the Mormon Empire. It also reaches into the Magic valley east of Twin Falls. Only the Pocatello area, a railroad, manufacturing, and university city, seems to break out of the cultural pull to Salt Lake City, the mecca of the Rocky Mountains. The Church of Jesus Christ of Latter-day Saints is the largest religious group in Idaho, and its adherents look to Salt Lake City for media, theological, economic, and, at times, political guidance.

For Boise, the state capital, it is a challenge to put together the elements of this divergent and divided state. While the rest of Idaho has grown very slowly, Boise is becoming a city of magnitude and force. Southwestern Idaho has maintained stronger allegiances to the state capital because of proximity and desire.

Even though national legislators had no idea what they

created in 1863, a greater possibility exists now than ever before that Idaho can become a united and unified state, proud of its natural environment and determined to leave a heritage of unsurpassed rivers, lakes, mountains, and resources. The native inhabitants, the American Indians, did not disturb the ecological balance, but it has taken a long time for Idaho to develop as a state able to contribute to the nation's history and to serve as an example to the United States of how to preserve a legacy for future generations.

2

Discovery and Exploration

T has been a long and difficult struggle for the American Indian. Indians never viewed their native domicile as an untamed wilderness or a frontier to be conquered. Their culture, customs, traditions, and religion were sacred and offered a historical and cultural heritage. The native Americans moved from area to area and lived off nature's bounties, occasionally clashing with another group. However, nothing could have prepared them for the shock of the white invasion of the nineteenth century. The disease and gunpowder frontier took its toll, and three hundred years after Jamestown, the native American civilization was struggling to retain a remote cultural identity.

In Idaho there were two major Indian groups, the Nez Percé in the north and the Shoshoni in the south. Simultaneously, bands of Kootenai and Coeur d'Alene Indians lived around Idaho's Panhandle, and northern Paiutes roamed through southwestern Idaho. Some of the Paiutes, called Bannocks, lived with the Shoshoni in southeastern Idaho. Other Shoshoni bands, Lemhis and Sheepeaters, lived in central Idaho, and are important to Idaho's history. These culturally and linguistically divergent groups comprise the historical and current Indians of Idaho. Like all American Indians, they are now citizens of the nation that moved them off Indian ancestral lands and determined that Indians must become like whites in order to survive and succeed.

The Shoshoni have been significant in Idaho's development from their first encounter with the Lewis and Clark expedition to the present. While the northern Idaho Indians trace their identity to the Pacific Coast, the Shoshoni and northern Paiute origins are not known exactly. They chose a difficult terrain but were able to utilize traditional subsistence skills. The Snake River valley became their homeland, and they moved up and down the tributaries in search of seeds, roots, and game. As seed gatherers, the Idaho Shoshoni utilized the flat, portable millstones. Grinding the various seeds and roots into flour enabled them to store greater quantities. While all Idaho Indians were noteworthy hunters, the Shoshoni were successful early as group hunters. Working together, they were able to hunt the buffalo and antelope in the southern part of Idaho. As these two meat staples disappeared, the mounted hunters moved eastward in search of the vanishing bison.

More has been written about the Nez Percé than any other Idaho Indian group for two reasons. In the first place, they also played a very significant role in the Lewis and Clark expedition. Secondly, much of the writing on Idaho-Indian history centers on the famous Nez Percé War of 1877 and Chief Joseph. Contrary to their French name, the Nez Percé did not pierce their noses, just as the Montana Flatheads did not flatten their heads. The Nez Percé remained off the main arteries of the westward movement, but retained an identity that fascinated explorers and travelers. Their sustenance was based on fish, roots, and the buffalo, in search for which they conducted annual forays across the Bitterroots. Gold miners eventually brought notoriety and confinement to the Nez Percé.

Before the reservations and the small permanent dwellings, these Indians were able to enjoy the wild animals, the wild streams, and the wild prairie roots of the vast openness of Idaho. Slowly, they moved from valley to mountain to river and back again. It was a hard, tedious existence, and the line between life and death was thin.

Although they were hunters, gatherers, and fishermen, Idaho's Indians maintained a traditional reverence for nature as their provider. Each individual developed power and self-control by ordering his behavior patterns. Taught to eat only as much as necessary and to hunt only what was needed, the Indians did not exploit the land nor the animals from which they gained food, clothing, and shelter. This individual and communal belief was like a religious manifestation, and it characterized Indian behavior for centuries. Then came a significant transportation and cultural revolution—the horse.

Some of the Indian respect for nature changed with the advent of the horse in the mid-eighteenth century. The horse, as an advance element of the white intrusion, reached Idaho long before the fair-skinned humans. Horses were probably brought into Idaho by the Shoshonis, who acquired them from the Comanches. Many groups began to adopt the culture of the mounted Plains Indians. Idaho Indians became knowledgeable about horse breeding and usage. Some experts speculate that northern Plains Indians, including the Blackfeet and Crow, obtained their first horses from Shoshonis and not from the southern plains. Because the horse offered a new mobility and a wider range of geographical contact, the effect on Idaho Indians was drastic.

After contact with the Plains Indians, the eastern Shoshoni and the northern Idaho groups were never the same. They now became both mobile bands of buffalo hunters and mounted warriors. Much of their culture and lifestyle was altered. Some began to live in the tipi; others stripped the slain animal and made jerky for storage; they began to adopt dances and ceremonies and headdresses from the Plains Indians; and skin or leather clothing was used. They also made skin containers instead of the willow and other basketry handicraft. Very importantly, Indians organized into bands greater than families and began to look to a chieftain to lead them on buffalo hunts and into battle.

These changes and alterations in culture and lifestyle affected Idaho Indians differently. Just as contemporary clothing style changes are felt in Boise long before they are in Riggins, so did the effect of the horse move slowly through Idaho. The new horse culture came to dominate the northern bands and many of the Shoshoni who resided in the northeastern part of the state. While the eastern Shoshoni were moving eastward into Wyoming and Montana for buffalo hunts, many of their kin in central and southwestern Idaho continued their old customs, gathering seeds and trapping fish and game, the new mobile life only affecting them modestly.

Horses competed for the grass and roots in desert areas, and the mountain bands originally had little use for the horse. Depending on what food they were pursuing that season or that year, the Shoshoni were often misnamed by outside observers. A "buffalo-eater" one year might be a "mountain sheep-cater" two years later, or "salmon-eaters" might find themselves "rabbit-eaters" the next spring or the "seed-eaters" could be the "pine-nut-eaters." What this means is that any given band went through a cyclical existence regarding their food supply. They lived on what was accessible and prepared for trips to augment their diet.

According to Shoshoni legend, there was an annual intertribal fair or rendezvous held near the place where the Weiser, Payette, and Boise rivers join the Snake. Indian people from throughout the Northwest gathered to trade and celebrate the beginning of the fishing time. The Nez Percé, who had become expert horse breeders, came to trade their ponies; while groups with Pacific Coast connections offered seashells and other ocean ornaments. The buffalo hunters brought hides and meat; while the northern Paiute had neat and precise arrowheads crafted from the obsidian of central Oregon. These trading fairs were replaced in the nineteenth century by white traders and their posts.

When the white fur trappers began to penetrate Idaho's mountain valleys in search of beaver, they found the Indians in a willing trading mood and seeking help against their enemies. Even prior to Lewis and Clark, the Blackfeet had begun to raid Shoshoni and Nez Percé villages in search of horses. Equipped with firearms obtained from British trappers, the Blackfeet were raising havoc among the Rocky Mountain Indian villages. Many of the Idaho Indian hunting parties became military bands as a protective measure. The Shoshoni were among the earliest to gain use of the horse, yet among the last to obtain firepower. It was well into the fur trading era before the Idaho Indians were armed and capable of holding their own against their kinsmen from the plains as well as white trappers.

Within the northern Rockies there was a magnificent natural setting, richly endowed with the resources of beaver, gold, water, and timber. A few thousand native Americans of various backgrounds moved freely along the rivers and through the mountain valleys. They often fought among themselves and developed keen animosities that would, in part, result in their eventual demise. As a new nation, headquartered twenty-five hundred miles away, began to flex its muscles and move westward, a clash between red and white was inevitable, but first came the never-ending conflict between nature and man.

Idaho's Shoshoni and Nez Percé had no idea of the forces unleashed by that small band of adventurers and explorers, under Lewis and Clark, who came seeking horses and guidance a century and three-quarters ago. The Rocky Mountain West was opened to American and British exploration, exploitation, and settlement, but the native inhabitants and their environment would be the most exploited and changed.

Thomas Jefferson wanted to explore the area from the Mississippi to the Pacific. Many early Americans dreamed of extending their prized republic from sea to sea, but Jefferson did something about it. Even before vast Louisiana was purchased, Jefferson prepared his secretary, Meriwether Lewis, for an expedition into the Northwest. The Lewis and Clark journey was a fantastic adventure of great significance to Idaho. By the time the explorers left Missouri, they realized most of the territory they were to explore had been purchased and was American. However, the expedition was literally a venture into the unknown and was much more hazardous, risky, and dangerous than contemporary space exploration. The Lewis and Clark expedition was only one in a series of adventures that gave whites knowledge of the mountain splendor of Idaho and the native Americans who lived in those high, peaceful alpine valleys and on the barren Snake River Plain. All of these explorers, trappers, and missionaries found that Idaho's rugged country was to be respected, admired, and, at times, feared. Lewis and Clark, the first whites known to have visited Idaho, learned that geographical fact early.

After fifteen months of exploration and discovery, thirty-one-year-old Meriwether Lewis and three of his companions gazed upon the western slope of the Rocky Mountains. At Lemhi Pass, they were 7,373 feet above sea level. To the east ran the waters that became the mighty Mississippi, and to the west were the streams that made the powerful Columbia. An intense student of botany, biology, and geography, Lewis had completed one of his goals—he had reached the Columbia watershed. From Lemhi Pass, the wandering adventurers looked westward across the vast mountain wilderness of Idaho, the last part to be seen by whites of what would become the forty-eight states. The towering snow-topped Bitterroots were succeeded by numerous mountain ranges that were much higher than any seen by Lewis before. In fact, for over a hundred miles west of the Lemhi valley, are the rugged mountains of central Idaho, many towering above ten thousand feet.

Lewis, thrilled by the knowledge that he had finally crossed the continental divide, hastily descended the western slope, which was much steeper than the eastern. After walking nearly a mile he came across "a handsome bold running Creek of Cold Clear water," where he recorded: "Here I first tasted the water of the great Columbia river." [1] Lewis and his partners then followed the stream, which became the Lemhi River, to the valley floor. Lewis had separated from the main party in order to find Shoshoni Indians and horses. Within one day after reaching Idaho, he located both. His initial fortunate experience in Idaho would not last. Idaho's geography and climate did not favor the Lewis and Clark expedition. The small party of whites discovered some Shoshonis along the river and, after persuading the Indians that they were not going to be destroyed, followed three Shoshoni women toward an Indian village. The small entourage was met by a band of mounted Indians, three of whom were

1. Meriwether Lewis and George Clark, *The Original Journals of Lewis and Clark,* ed. Reuben G. Thwaites, Antiquarian Edition, 7 vols. (New York: Antiquarian Press, 1959), 2:334.

armed with small rifles, which Lewis speculated had been obtained from British trappers. Lewis left his rifle behind and courageously advanced toward the Indians, accompanied by the women and carrying a flag. The women told their story to the Shoshoni chief, and the braves dismounted and gave Lewis a cordial reception, which consisted of a bear hug from every Indian. The whites then sat surrounded by the Shoshoni and smoked a pipe of friendship.

The intruders were treated well by these Shoshonis and their chief, Cameahwait. Lewis stayed with them in their village for two nights and a day and learned a great deal about the Shoshoni and the Idaho portion of the road ahead of him. The Virginia-born Lewis was very impressed with the caliber of horses owned by the Shoshoni, and noticed that several had Spanish brands. He also observed that some bridles and bits, as well as the mules, were of Spanish origin. Through one of Lewis's companions, George Drouillard, Cameahwait answered Lewis's inquiries concerning how the Lemhi River made its way to the Columbia. It was learned that the Lemhi flowed into a much larger stream, the Salmon, and that it was totally impossible to navigate these streams to the Pacific-bound Columbia, nor feasible to travel down the larger Salmon River Canyon by land. Although Lewis hoped that the Shoshoni chief was exaggerating the difficulty of the Salmon River gorge, it was not good news—especially when the white explorers found that Cameahwait had told the truth when describing the "River of No Return."

Lewis persuaded many of the Shoshonis to accompany him with extra horses back across Lemhi Pass to join William Clark and the rest of the expedition. When Clark finally arrived, it was discovered that Cameahwait and Sacajawea, the Shoshoni girl who traveled with Lewis and Clark, were brother and sister. This lucky fact of kinship aided in the horse trades that ensued. The next morning Clark and eleven men left to find out if there was a feasible path to the Columbia River down the Salmon River. After constructing some caches, and making pack-saddles, Lewis crossed once again into Idaho to see what Clark discovered.

William Clark, redheaded and thirty-five years old, made a most wise decision. After tracing the Lemhi River to the Salmon, which he called Lewis's River, he went down the Salmon for about fifty miles. He concluded the obvious—a canoe trip down the Salmon River would be disastrous and to attempt the canyon on horseback would be certain folly. Clark described the terrain he saw in his journal:

> [t]he Mountains [are] Close and is a perpendicular clift on each Side, and Continues for a great distance and that the water runs with great violence from one rock to the other on each side foaming & roreing thro rocks in every direction, So as to render the passage of any thing impossible.[2]

Clark and his Shoshoni guides described the Salmon River and its canyon very well. The mountains and the river were impassable and Clark also doubted that the rugged area could provide enough food. He dispatched John Colter back to Lewis with the suggestion that they move north with Shoshoni guides and horses and find another branch of the Columbia. Although the recrossing of the Bitterroots would be difficult and time-consuming, Clark's recommendation undoubtedly saved the expedition from a tragedy in central Idaho.

Traveling north was not any easier. They moved up the North Fork of the Salmon River and eventually crossed back into what is now Montana near the Lost Trail Pass. The precipitous mountain trail caused pack horses to lose their footing and tumble down the slopes, spreading their load throughout the heavy timber. Snow fell around the first of September, and food rations were nearly depleted. Four of the six Indian guides turned back, leaving Toby, who had accompanied Clark down the Salmon, and one of his sons.

A week later, the expedition once again began an ascent over the Bitterroots. This time they chose a pass, Lolo, which is nearly 5,200 feet in elevation and approximately two hundred miles north and a little west of Lemhi Pass. It was a road traveled by the Nez Percé Indians when they went east in search of buffalo. Cameahwait had warned Lewis that the road was a very bad one and that there was little game. Even this warning could not have prepared the expedition for the rugged Clearwater Mountains. From the time they began to climb up the eastern slope until they passed through the mountains, it would take eleven long, difficult, and distressing days. These mountains in Idaho would cause them hunger, cold, pain, and exhaustion, and the adventurers would suffer as much hardship as at any other place on the entire trip.

The explorers crossed into Idaho again on September 13, and camped at the lower end of a meadow surrounded by mountains. The next day it rained intermittently, with the rain changing periodically to sleet and snow. In this storm, the expedition made a wrong turn and lost the trail. They had followed a creek that ultimately became the Lochsa River, but the Nez Percé trail remained on a high ridge. To make matters worse, the hunters had only killed two or three grouse, and when over thirty hungry men needed a meal, three grouse would hardly suffice. Lewis concluded that it would be necessary to kill a colt, and that sustained the travelers for another day. After another week of early snow, lost trails, and short rations, the last colt was shot and a general mood of despair prevailed. Lewis and Clark decided that Clark and six hunters should push ahead in search of game and a way out of the mountains. The seriousness of the situation and a testament to the leadership of Lewis and Clark is the fact that on that day, September 18, Clark and his six hunters ate nothing—while Lewis and those behind dined on pre-mixed portable soup made with snow, bear oil, and twenty candles. They were not yet ready to eat all of their saddle and pack horses. Sometime during the day, Clark saw the plains in the distance and realized that the end was within reach. It is ironic to note that although Lewis and Clark were traversing some of the most spectacular mountain scenery Idaho has to offer, the trees, creeks, gorges, and valleys were not described. Each physical feature was another barrier to cross or avoid. The snowcapped peaks, tall green pines, and crystal clear brooks were not unnoticed, they just were not appreciated!

On Friday, September 20, William Clark finally arrived at Weippe Prairie. Shortly thereafter, he discovered a Nez Percé village and dined on salmon and camas root. After staying one night, he descended from the prairie to the Clearwater River and met Twisted Hair, a Nez Percé chief. Clark and the hunters then awaited the arrival of the later force under Lewis. Lewis and his men spent a great deal of time rounding up horses each morning, and after existing on meals of crayfish, grouse, and coyote, finally caught up with Clark on 22 September. That evening an exhausted, yet relieved Lewis, once again exuded confidence as he wrote:

> the pleasure I now felt in having triumphed over the Rocky
> Mountains and descending once more to a level and fertile country
> where there was every rational hope of finding a comfortable
> subsistence for myself and party can be more readily conceived than
> expressed, nor was the flattering prospect of the final success of the
> expedition less pleasing.[3]

Meriwether Lewis realized that the mountains deserved the respect of the expedition, especially as he contemplated next spring's return trip.

On October 7, nearly two months after crossing Lemhi Pass and almost a month since starting over Lolo, the expedition boarded canoes and began the trip down the Clearwater. Leaving their branded horses, saddles, and some cached ammunition behind, they tried their luck with Idaho's rivers. After a couple of accidents while running rapids, Lewis and Clark decided to be a little more patient and to portage around the difficult places. Three days after launching the canoes, they arrived at the confluence of the Snake and Clearwater at present-day Lewiston, Idaho. Clark was accurately convinced that the Snake River contained the waters of the river they had explored in mid-August, the Salmon. He called both the Salmon and the Snake "Lewis's River," but the name of the explorer did not survive as his partner in discovery had wished.

As white discoverers of what became Idaho, Lewis and Clark left a lasting impact on the area. They met the Shoshoni and the Nez Percé and were able to establish friendly, co-operative relations. They had experienced and survived the rugged mountain

---

3. Thwaites, *Original Journals of Lewis and Clark,* 3:83.

wilderness. In fact, they had finally crossed the state through an area that is still much as it was when the expedition stumbled through. There is not an easy way across central or northern Idaho. When Lewis and Clark returned the following spring, Idaho's mountains were still ominous and uninviting.

Anxious to return and report to Thomas Jefferson, Lewis and Clark left the Pacific Coast as soon as spring 1806 arrived, and by early May were back in Nez Percé country. After some difficulty, they obtained most of their horses and caches and prepared to recross the Clearwater and Bitterroot mountains. The Nez Percé chiefs had advised the explorers to wait until at least June and preferably later to avoid being in thick wet snow. Once again, the weary men were discouraged. After a day spent traveling up the Clearwater through eight inches of new snow, Lewis and Clark decided to select a campsite and await a true Idaho spring.

The explorers remained at this site, near Kamiah, Idaho, for nearly a month, spending the time in physical and mental preparation for the mountain assault. Except for the time spent in their winter quarters, they remained at this camp longer than at any other. It was a decision of necessity, not of desire. Kamiah was a good hunting area, and there was excellent pasture for the horses. Each day hunting parties were dispatched and the Nez Percé traded roots and other foods for a variety of trinkets. Many of the men once more became sick, including York, Clark's black servant. While at Kamiah, they increased their horse herd considerably as well as adding to the meat supply. By June 10, the expedition was ready to leave the Clearwater and begin the eastward trek. They attempted to persuade some Nez Percé to accompany them as guides, but the knowledgeable Indians said it was still too early and the snow would be very deep.

Confident that June 10 was summer, and deceived by the warm weather along the Clearwater, Lewis and Clark left Kamiah and climbed out of the canyon to the Weippe Prairie. For four days they hunted and further prepared to cross the mountains. The beautiful camas was in bloom and the light blue petals gave the prairie the appearance of a rippling lake. Although it rained, the hunters had considerable success, so on June 15, the ascent of the Clearwater Mountains began, with George Drouillard as guide.

From the first day on, Idaho's mountains and trees and weather seemed to conspire against the expedition. Once on top of a ridge, Clark stopped to view the mountains to the south, north, and east of them. He observed that those high rugged peaks were still very much covered by snow. For two more days the horseback caravan slowly moved up the mountains, but soon they discovered eight to ten feet of snow covering the trail. Drouillard found it increasingly difficult to locate the path. Finally at lunchtime on 17 June, Lewis and Clark made the decision to return to Weippe Prairie, secure Nez Percé guides, and wait for more of the snow to melt. After constructing a high scaffold and putting a good deal of their food and baggage on it, the explorers retreated for the first time on their expedition. Idaho's uninviting mountain wilderness had achieved a temporary victory.

A week later, heavily provisioned and accompanied by three young Nez Percé men, the expedition again set out in a northeasterly direction. The Indian guides' knowledge of the trail and the fact that some of the snow had melted made the second assault relatively easy. Lewis and Clark both admitted that without their guides, they could have easily become forever lost in the vast sea of snowcapped mountain ranges. The deep and hard-packed snow enabled the horses to move over fallen timbers, rocks, and other hazards with some ease. It only took the party six days to cross the mountains and reach the continental divide. It was apparently an unusually late winter, but the return trip was safely executed. On June 29, they crossed to the eastern slope of the Rockies, leaving Idaho with the realization that they had finally conquered the great Rocky Mountain barrier.

After spending parts of four months in what became Idaho, the expedition left, but their impact was deeply felt. They had established friendly relations with two great Indian nations, the Shoshoni and the Nez Percé. They demonstrated that a route through the northern Rockies to the Pacific Coast was difficult. Subsequent travelers would seek an alternate route, rather than hazard the Idaho mountains, canyons, and streams. Their expedition paved the way for the developing Missouri valley fur trade's penetration of the Rockies. In fact, once the expedition began its descent down the Missouri, it met traders moving toward the Rockies, and one of the members of the expedition, John Colter, received permission to go back up the river immediately. This led to Colter's fame as the discoverer of Yellowstone National Park. The government-sponsored Lewis and Clark expedition also gave the United States a strong and valid claim to the Oregon Country, of which Idaho was a part. In reality, the expedition opened the way for successive waves of trappers, missionaries, and other explorers to participate in the Idaho adventure.

It is essential to realize that for four decades after discovery, Idaho was disputed territory. At first, Spain, Russia, Great Britain, and the United States all claimed parts of the Oregon Country. The Spanish ceded their claims to the Oregon Country in 1819, and the Russians withdrew to Alaska by 1825. This left the United States and Great Britain as the principal claimants, and much of their jockeying for position took place throughout Idaho. Exploring expeditions and trapping companies representing both nations crisscrossed Idaho, each seeking Indian allies to use against the other. The drama of Idaho after Lewis and Clark is set on a stage of international intrigue and competition, and Idaho continued to play a role as Americans sought their "manifest destiny."

The fur trappers were an interesting breed of men whose only law was that of survival. The American trappers usually moved as small groups into the wilderness and reappeared for what evolved as an annual summer rendezvous. The British liked to establish trading houses and have the Indians come to them, but that system did not succeed in the Rocky Mountains as it had in the upper Midwest. So the representatives of Hudson's Bay would put together an expedition of company men, freemen under contract, Indian wives, children, and baggage. Their entourage often had the appearance of a nomadic village. The Americans and the British were constantly trying to outwit or contain each other. Continually competing, they tried to cultivate the various

Indian tribes, steal rival caches, and confuse one another. The various private companies of the two nations played out their little cold war until the early 1840s.

A good percentage of the men who went into the mountains in search of beaver were conquered by the harsh environment. They lived in constant danger and—although many seemed to revel in crisis—the barren land, early snow, jagged cliffs, raging rapids, late snow, and Indian resistance destroyed a good percentage of the trappers. Andrew Henry lost twenty-seven men on his first trip into Idaho and, according to one source, Nathaniel Wyeth, who founded Fort Hall, salvaged only forty men out of two hundred after three years in the mountains. Many of the trappers adopted the methods and lifestyle of the Indians. They lived with Indian women and fathered numerous children. In order to survive, they tricked while they traded and stole if desperate. Death and hunger were constant companions; yet, the lure of the mountain wilderness was powerfully magnetic. The mountain man led an elemental life of eating and sleeping and slaying. Thousands of beaver were killed for their pelts as a consequence of the trappers' intrusion. After a stream was trapped, it meant a new area had to be found—thus, the constant penetration of difficult canyons and different valleys and virgin rivers. So long as the beaver pelts had great value, it was inevitable that the trappers would pursue the animal across the continent.

The British fur trappers and traders were not far behind the American explorers. Although there were many competing British and American concerns, David Thompson of the North West Company first penetrated the Panhandle of Idaho in the spring of 1808 and set up a trading house at Bonners Ferry among the Kootenai Indians. Thompson, a most interesting Welshman, seemed as interested in geography and cartography as he was in trading. The short, compactly built trader was a unique individual who refused to trade alcohol for furs. He had married a fourteen-year-old Indian girl ten years earlier, and she and their three small children accompanied him into Idaho. In the late summer of 1809, Thompson constructed Kullyspell House on the eastern shore of Lake Pend Oreille. For four years, Thompson and his associates traveled back and forth along the Idaho and Montana tributaries of the Columbia. After charting the entire area from the source of the Columbia to the mouth, Thompson abandoned Kullyspell House and the Indians of the Panhandle. British trappers continued to trade in northern Idaho, but the North West Company had taken their booty and moved on. Thompson knew that Americans were also invading the area, but the British government seemed unable to assist him in keeping Americans out of the Oregon Country. When Thompson arrived at the mouth of the Columbia in 1811, he found Americans already there. By the time Thompson left Idaho, two other major groups of American trappers had entered the state and those in the employ of John Jacob Astor had crossed the difficult terrain.

In the spring of 1810, Andrew Henry and some of Manuel Lisa's Missouri Fur Company trappers had crossed into eastern Idaho from Montana after a skirmish with Blackfeet Indians. They established a camp on Henry's Fork of the Snake River. One winter in the upper Snake River valley did not create an intense desire among the trappers to establish themselves permanently; so in the spring of 1811, they split into three groups and left the area completely. Later, in the fall of that year, the overland Astorians briefly visited the same area. John Jacob Astor, a wealthy entrepreneur, attempted to construct a fur trading empire in the Northwest. Using many of the old British North Westers as partners, he decided to establish simultaneously a fort at the mouth of the Columbia by sea and send an overland exploring expedition. In economic and human terms, the venture was a tragic disaster. However, from the point of view of Idaho history, the overland Astorians of 1811 and the returning Astorians of 1812 were quite significant as explorers. They experienced repeated disasters, and some died within Idaho because the Snake River country was so inhospitable.

Wilson Price Hunt, an American partner of Astor, was the leader of Astor's overland expedition. Because of the intense trading rivalry with Manuel Lisa on the upper Missouri River, Hunt left the friendly waters of the Missouri, secured horses, and moved overland through northern Wyoming. After crossing the Big Horn and Wind River mountains, the Astorians saw the Tetons. The Hunt party crossed the continental divide at Union Pass, one of the highest passes in the Rockies, and moved toward the headwaters of the Snake. After traversing Teton Pass and crossing into Idaho, they stopped at the site of Henry's Fort. It was now October 1811, and as Hunt and his companions viewed the snowy peaks around them, they should have gone into winter quarters. Instead, they abandoned their horses, built crude canoes, named the Snake River the Canoe River, and pushed off toward the Columbia. Hunt had no knowledge of the Snake River gorges and Hells Canyon. Two and one-half weeks later, the middle Snake rapids had taken their toll, and the Astorians were forced to walk the remainder of the way through Idaho. Hunt split his expedition into three groups as they attempted to push on to the Columbia. Hunt continued to follow the Snake to Hells Canyon and then turned west to cross the Blue Mountains to the Columbia; others, under the leadership of Donald MacKenzie, went north along the Snake River and eventually reached the Clearwater River, where they built a small post. Later, MacKenzie's group followed this river down the Lewis and Clark path to Astoria. At least four of the overland Astorians had died, and, although they had pursued a course over much of what was to become the Oregon Trail through Idaho, the memories of the Snake were unpleasant. It is interesting that Marie Dorian, the pregnant wife of one of the French-Canadian trappers, survived the crossing, although her baby, born during the journey, only lived ten days.

The next spring, another Astor partner, Robert Stuart, was selected to return to the East with news of the expedition. With five companions, he retraced Hunt's path up the Columbia, across eastern Oregon and to the Snake in Idaho. Stuart was robbed of his horse by an Indian, but the party pushed on upriver. They came across four Astorians who had been left to trap in eastern Idaho, and the enlarged expedition continued on in search of a better pass through the Rockies. When Stuart reached the confluence of the Portneuf River and the Snake, near the later site of Fort Hall, he left the Snake and turned toward the Bear River valley. Deciding not to return to the East, three of the group left and resumed their trapping. Unknowingly, Stuart was close to the discovery of South Pass, the easiest way across the continental divide. If he could have followed the Bear for a distance and then traversed a small sagebrush plateau to the Green, he would have been able to cross to the eastern slope without difficulty. This good fortune was too much to expect for the hard-luck Astorians. Stuart was turned back by a band of Crow Indians who eventually stole all of the whites' horses. It took another month of wandering through eastern Idaho before Stuart was able to find the Green River and eventually South Pass. Basically, Robert Stuart had followed the path that was to become the Oregon Trail.

Astor's total northwestern adventure finally was sold to the British North West Company for about one-fifth of what Astor claimed it was worth. Yet, the Astorians in Idaho had still other tragedies. John Reid, a clerk, led an expedition of nine men into the Boise River country in the fall of 1813. Six of them were killed by Bannock Indians, who were infuriated when the Astorians hanged an Indian for petty theft. Only Marie Dorian and her two children escaped death, but her husband was one of those struck down. Later a group of trappers under Donald MacKenzie, including some Hawaiians, were lost and believed killed in southwestern Idaho. That area was later referred to as Owyhee, which is the earlier spelling of Hawaii. The friendly relations Lewis and Clark had achieved with Idaho's Indians were destroyed by the subsequent trappers and explorers who came to exploit and deplete.

After the Astorians and Henry's men temporarily left Idaho, the area was open for a decade of British exploitation. Americans who returned east knew more of the geography and hazards, but it would take some time for an organized American effort to combat the representatives of the Hudson's Bay Company, which had merged with the North West Company. Another problem was developing as well. After an area was trapped out, it was necessary to penetrate unexplored terrain immediately. This fact forced the British trappers into the mountains of all of Idaho. Once again, the Indians and nature combatted these encroachments, but the British altered their tactics successfully.

Gigantic Donald MacKenzie, one of the original overland Astorians, had gone to work for the rival North West Company after Astor's fur scheme collapsed. Weighing nearly three hundred pounds, MacKenzie threw his mind and body into a plan that would eventually carry him throughout Idaho and into Wyoming and Utah. From the mouth of the Snake, at Fort Nez Perce, for three successive years MacKenzie led expeditions into the Snake River country. Prior to this time, the basis of the British fur trade had been manipulation of the native Americans. Once the Indians became dependent on white goods, they would come to the trading posts loaded with pelts. This system simply did not work in the Rocky Mountains. The mountain Indians did not enjoy trapping and were reluctant to alter their lifestyle. MacKenzie decided that the Hudson's Bay trappers would have to get the pelts themselves, as the Americans had been doing east of the Rockies. There was one notable exception. The Americans had always been willing to go about in small all-male groups, but not the British companies.

MacKenzie moved French-Canadian *voyageurs,* Iroquois trappers, wigwams, dogs, children, and women into Idaho in 1818. MacKenzie's men roamed as far south as the Bear River and Bear Lake, and as far east as Wyoming's Green River. They trapped nearly all of the tributaries of the Snake. They explored and named countless rivers and streams including Pierre's Hole, or the Teton Valley. Supplied by horses from Fort Nez Perce on the Snake, MacKenzie succeeded in the field for three years. His horses, coming and going across southern Idaho, beat a path that within a few years would become part of the Oregon Trail. Each year MacKenzie's horse caravans would return with thousands of beaver pelts.

This intense exploitation of the Snake River streams was prompted by international as well as economic motives. The United States and Great Britain, unable to settle on a boundary line in the Northwest, in 1818 agreed upon joint occupation of the area for ten years. The British knew that one way to drive the Americans away was to deplete their economic supply—the beaver. If they could get the beaver first, then, they reasoned, the greedy Yankees would turn their attention to the Southwest. Year after year, the British expeditions went southward with the goal of depleting the streams to keep the American trappers on the eastern slope of the Rockies. By the early 1820s, it appeared that the British scheme was working, but Idaho remained a battleground.

After MacKenzie's Snake expeditions, the two British companies merged, and MacKenzie was sent to Manitoba. He was replaced by Michael Bourdon in 1822 and Finnan McDonald in 1823. Bourdon, who had been one of the MacKenzie men who penetrated the Bear Lake country, had had a horrendous year in Idaho. Starting from a base in Montana, he managed to get as far south as the Blackfoot River, where he lost some of his men in a skirmish with Blackfeet Indians, and fourteen trappers and their women deserted him. Bourdon had to cache nearly seven hundred beaver pelts. The following year, Bourdon returned, but the red-whiskered six-foot four-inch Finnan McDonald was now the leader.

McDonald had been with David Thompson at the founding of Kullyspell House in 1809. Now with a new group of trappers, he set out once again to trap in Idaho and recover Bourdon's cache. Near Lemhi Pass, the trappers were ambushed by Blackfeet Indians. After losing a number of men, including Bourdon, the Hudson's Bay trappers surrounded the Blackfeet in a thicket and set fire to it. This battle was perhaps the most decisive Canadian fur trappers fought against Indians in the Northwest. For a few years, the Blackfeet were much less aggressive while on their Idaho forays. McDonald obtained more than four thousand furs, but his repeated skirmishes with the Blackfeet caused him to weary of his leadership of the Snake River expedition. He proceeded as far south as the Bear and then moved into the northern Teton Valley before leaving the state, via Lemhi Pass.

Eighteen twenty-four was a pivotal year in the history of Idaho, the Northwest, and the fur trade. After nearly a decade of remaining east of the Rockies, the Americans were again moving onto the western slope. Andrew Henry, William Ashley, and Jedediah Smith were only a few of the Americans chasing the beaver. After losing many men and concluding that the hazards were too risky on the Missouri, Ashley dispatched Smith to the south with the charge that he and his men trap the Columbia system. In the winter of 1823–1824, this small group crossed South Pass from the east and trapped the Green River. After a heavy catch, Smith's party split, with some taking the furs east and the rest moving from the Green to the Bear River. South Pass to the Bear—the last link in what was to become the Oregon Trail had been forged. Now Smith moved into Idaho for an inevitable collision with the Hudson's Bay Snake River expedition.

Alexander Ross, another British Astorian, led the Hudson's Bay 1824 excursion into Idaho. Although Ross did not do as well as he had hoped economically, diplomatically the venture was most significant. Ross led a strange caravan of hundreds, including representatives of eleven different Indian tribes, across the Lemhi Pass in April. Internal problems caused the expedition to fracture, and some Iroquois went toward the Snake while Ross and most of the people began a difficult trapping and exploring course through central Idaho. Conscious of the Blackfeet presence, they kept to the mountains and were the first to trap the Wood River near present Sun Valley. Finally, Ross led his followers around the Smoky and Soldier mountains to the Boise River. While in this area, they trapped also the Weiser and Payette rivers of western Idaho. The return journey took Ross into the Sawtooth Mountains and Stanley Basin. Surrounded by numerous 10,000-foot peaks, Ross explored the headwaters of the Salmon and its famed Middle Fork. The trappers eventually made their way back to their cache near Challis, but the Iroquois furmen had not yet arrived.

The free Iroquois had considerable success in trapping, but were robbed of their guns, horses, and some pelts by marauding Bannocks. Near the spot where the Blackfoot River joins the Snake, Jedediah Smith and six other Americans found the defenseless Iroquois party. Smith, who wanted to study British trapping patterns, agreed to escort the Iroquois back to Ross for the price of their pelts. So in October 1824, Ross was joined by

the Americans as he left Idaho to return to Flathead House.
Ross knew that the presence of Smith would cause him trouble,
but the Americans had rescued the Iroquois. Acting against his
better judgment, Ross permitted Smith to accompany him to the
Hudson's Bay post.

After a sojourn of a month at the post, Smith's group joined
Peter Skene Ogden, who had replaced Ross, for the next year's
hunt. Ogden, a tenacious stocky man, was vehement in his de-
nunciation of Ross for allowing Smith to penetrate British controlled areas. As the cumbersome group moved into Idaho to
begin trapping, Smith left and began to trap the streams in advance of Ogden. He followed this pattern all the way past the
42nd parallel, or the southern boundary of Idaho. As Ogden followed the Bear to the Great Salt Lake, he ran into other Americans, as well as traders from Taos. The Americans tried to
threaten the British by claiming that Ogden was on American
soil, but both parties were in Mexico.

It was clear that the eastern and southern borders of Idaho
were the battlegrounds for beaver pelts. The British did not
want the Americans to press farther west and continued their
exploitation of the beaver. The Americans, naive about the
schemes of the British, also killed any beaver in sight without
concern for the future. Their goal, too, seemed to be to get there
first and get the furs before the British could compete. Neither
nation's representatives were concerned with ecology, conservation, or preservation.

The determined mountainmen pushed on and into new country. American furmen encountered the English throughout
Idaho, yet they never controlled much of Idaho. Each year more
territory was explored and trapped. The American-developed
rendezvous system aided in limiting trappers to the mountains
and keeping them well supplied. All of northern Idaho was controlled by Hudson's Bay and the British trapped most of the
rest. No rendezvous was ever held deeper inside the Oregon
Country than the Teton Valley, or old Pierre's Hole, west of the
Tetons. Jedediah Smith, Donald Jackson, and William Sublette
tried to develop more trade to the west, but the Hudson's Bay
Company strategy paid off. By the late 1820s most of the acces-

sible Idaho streams were trapped out and the Americans contented themselves in western Wyoming. Numerous American and British trappers had crisscrossed Idaho and knew the hazards of its terrain. After two decades of continual competition, it appeared that the Oregon Country was apt to remain British. However, by 1832 other elements were entering to play a part in Idaho's future—more fur companies, the Christian missionaries, and American military exploring expeditions.

Nathaniel Wyeth and Benjamin L. E. Bonneville were important figures in this stage of the struggle. Wyeth, about thirty, was a junior partner in a Massachusetts ice company near Boston. Bonneville, thirty-five, short, heavy, and prematurely bald, was a graduate of West Point and a captain in the U. S. Army. Acting separately, the two men devised schemes designed to control the American fur trade. Wyeth was convinced that any successful enterprise needed to be provisioned from the sea, and Bonneville believed, as some trappers had written, that wagons, bearing supplies, could be pulled into the mountains. Wyeth talked his way into the veteran William Sublette's caravan, while Bonneville tried it alone. In May 1832, the two expeditions left Independence, Missouri.

Wyeth and Sublette entered Idaho near Pierre's Hole for the annual rendezvous. During the rendezvous, in spite of the fact that Sublette had brought 450 gallons of straight alcohol for the festivities, nearly half of Wyeth's men voted to resign and return to New England. To make matters worse it was at this 1832 rendezvous that the trappers and the Gros Ventre Indians, allies of the Blackfeet, did battle in the beautiful Teton Valley, and nearly forty were killed on both sides. Wyeth moved south to the Snake and first viewed the territory where later he would establish Fort Hall. Throughout the summer Wyeth's party trapped the semidesolate mountains along the Idaho-Utah border. By fall, they were on their way to the Columbia and the anticipated union with the ship Wyeth had sent around Cape Horn. The ship never came, and Wyeth was forced to live off the good graces of John McLoughlin at the Hudson's Bay post, Fort Vancouver. By the next year, the entire Wyeth venture had collapsed.

Bonneville, on leave from the army, never did reach the rendezvous at Pierre's Hole. The wagons bounced along through South Pass into western Wyoming. Many of his trappers quit and joined other expeditions while others were enticed to remain to accompany him. As fall approached, Bonneville constructed a stockade on the Salmon and parked the wagons. The captain dispatched his trappers for a winter hunt, but many were killed and twenty took their horses, traps, and pelts and joined the Crow Indians. With Wyeth in his bosom, and Bonneville floundering in eastern Idaho, John McLoughlin, the Hudson's Bay factor, could hardly have been worried.

Although Wyeth and Bonneville were failures as trappers and businessmen, their activities did a great deal to publicize the Oregon Country. While the bald Captain Bonneville explored much of the Snake River valley and faced numerous geographical hazards, in the process he rarely caught beaver. His adventures as chronicled by Washington Irving became widely circulated. Insofar as Bonneville's impact on Idaho is concerned, it can be said that he stimulated an appreciation of the Bear River valley as a potential provisioning point for Oregon-bound travelers, and he also became convinced, as the Astorians had been, that it was impossible to go down the Snake River into Hells Canyon. His dream of quick riches was shattered in Idaho's mountains, and Bonneville returned to his career in the regular army.

Wyeth's importance is of greater note because of the creation of Fort Hall in 1834, and because he brought Protestant missionaries, and their belongings, across the entire Oregon Trail. Although Wyeth's dream of supplying the fur trade from the mouth of the Columbia to his post at Fort Hall never materialized, the existence of Fort Hall aided the next wave of westerners. In fact, Wyeth's post led Thomas McKay of the Hudson's Bay Company to construct a similar operation at Fort Boise in far western Idaho. Thus, during 1834, the main recuperating and provisioning posts along the Oregon Trail were constructed because of the fur trade rivalries. Three years later, a disgruntled Wyeth sold his post on the Snake River to the Hudson's Bay Company and left for Boston. As the beaver pelt became simultaneously harder to obtain and of similar value to a buffalo robe, the hardy mountainmen witnessed caravans of missionaries and settlers traveling the roads that trappers and Indians had made into paths. By 1840, many of the vagabond trappers had become guides, others hunted the buffalo, and some drifted east or west into farming life. Few stayed in the Idaho mountains they explored or in the river valleys they had trapped. Settling was left to another type of frontiersmen.

Missionaries came in all kinds and from many denominations. Their original motivation for coming into Idaho was the belief that the Nez Percé and Flatheads wanted the Christian religion. This myth developed from an 1831 visit by Indian representatives to Saint Louis. There was also a great concern on the part of religious denominations for the trapper and his half-breed offspring. The driving forces of missionary zeal and cheap Oregon land brought Christianity in a variety of forms into Idaho.

Jason Lee, a New England Methodist, had accompanied Nathaniel Wyeth on Wyeth's second journey into the West in 1834. In fact, Lee conducted a religious service at Fort Hall the Sunday they encamped there. Following the sermon, a horse race resulted in the death of a French-Canadian trapper. As if to typify future competitive proselyting problems, the trapper was given a Catholic, Protestant, and Indian funeral. He was, in the words of Wyeth, "well buried." Lee and his followers ultimately settled the Willamette Valley, and he became a leading force in advertising and propagandizing the virtues of the Oregon Country south of the Columbia. The good missionary was not at all tempted by the sagebrush-covered Snake River Plain in Idaho.

The American Board of Foreign Missions, representing Presbyterians and Congregationalists, was only a year behind Lee. Samuel Parker, a middle-aged dreamer, recruited a chunky, round-headed doctor, Marcus Whitman, and away they went into the Rocky Mountains. Joining the American Fur Company's annual brigade, the missionaries and trappers traveled together to the Green River. Whitman's medical experience spared the missionaries from continual ridicule by the trappers, and a quick observation told God's representatives that the religious field was ready to harvest. Parker pushed on through Idaho and Whitman returned East to drum up new support from the mission board. While Parker tried to teach the Sermon on the Mount and the Ten Commandments and monogamy, Whitman prepared for an assault the next year.

Whitman married the tall blonde Narcissa Prentiss, to whom the Reverend Henry H. Spalding had once proposed. Spurned, Spalding had persuaded Eliza Hart, by mail, to be his life's companion. Now the Whitmans and Spaldings were preparing to travel across the continent together, sharing the same wagon and tent, on a journey that was also to be the Whitmans' honeymoon. Spalding and Whitman proved rather incompatible, and to make matters more disconcerting, by the time their wagon reached Idaho, Narcissa was pregnant.

Eliza Spalding and Narcissa Whitman were the first white women to cross the continent. Although they took a wagon most of the way, it was a miserable, difficult journey. Day after day through Idaho, the grinding routine almost drove them and their husbands to the breaking point. At one point, Narcissa complained about the distance, but quickly chastised herself. The mosquitoes along the Portneuf were noted as well as the stiff and hard sagebrush along the Snake. Twice in Idaho, at Fort Hall and Fort Boise, they washed their clothes and relaxed. Once into Oregon and nearer their destination, spirits brightened considerably.

Henry and Eliza Spalding returned to Idaho later that winter and built a house and school in Nez Percé country at Lapwai, ten miles above the confluence of the Snake and Clearwater rivers. As a pair of missionaries, they were unusually patient, tolerant, and wise—wise, because they spent more time on home economics, agriculture, and practical living than on religion. Convinced that inevitable white encroachment would destroy the buffalo herds and other game, Spalding wanted to teach the nomadic Nez Percé to try farming, and for this purpose he acquired seed for various crops. Subsequent missionaries, especially Asa B. Smith, who opened a station at Kamiah, disagreed with Spalding's methods. The debate became public, and the entire mission was almost terminated because of it. Whitman's hasty crosscountry journey and the subsequent resolution of differences saved Lapwai. Spalding had a corn mill, sawmill, printing press, and school in operation. He even diverted the creek to irrigate crops during a hot summer. Only in efforts to convert all of the Nez Percé did the Spaldings experience failure. After the Whitman Massacre of 1847, the Spaldings were forced to retreat until the 1860s, when they moved back into Idaho territory. One of the reasons for their proselyting difficulty was the fact that Roman Catholic priests were also in the area.

The Jesuit brothers moved in among the Coeur d'Alenes and Kootenai shortly after Spalding settled Lapwai. Father Pierre-Jean De Smet visited the area in 1840 and outlined the plans for missionary activities. Father Nicholas Point selected a mission site on the Saint Joe River near Saint Maries during the winter of 1842. Catholic Iroquois trappers had prepared the Coeur d'Alenes for the ritual and procedures of the church. Consequently, the Jesuits experienced some success with the Indians, even though Father Point despised the Indians' dirtiness, idolatry, gluttony, gambling, and "moral abandonment." By 1844, Point claimed to have baptized two-thirds of their number and noted that there was a remarkable change among the tribe. In 1846 Father Joseph Hoset moved the entire mission and Indian followers some twenty miles from Lake Coeur d'Alene to a site later called Cataldo. Several years later the Indians constructed an impressive church building at Cataldo, the Sacred Heart Mission.

The Christian missionaries ultimately were made to appear as hypocrites. Treaties added confusion upon confusion as broken pacts became the order of the day. When soldiers were brought in to move Indians, they rarely appeared to be individuals worthy of emulation. The brotherhood and goodwill preached by the well-intentioned missionaries were usually a joke to the military representatives of the government. Indians were no longer necessary for physical survival as they had been to Lewis and Clark, or for economic success as they had been to the trappers, or for a fulfillment of missionary idealism. However, the missionaries did play a significant part in stimulating interest in the Pacific Northwest. The movement of thousands of Americans into Oregon ultimately solved the British-American dispute over ownership.

Two pivotal decision points of the Oregon Trail were in Idaho. At Fort Hall, most westward-bound pioneers made the decision—to Oregon or California. If it was California, they followed the Oregon Trail for a short distance and then crossed to the Raft River, skirting the southern boundary of the state where Wyeth had earlier trapped. After passing City of Rocks, a great natural landmark, they dipped into the Utah-Nevada area and sought the Humboldt River. If Oregon was their choice, wagons followed the Snake across the remainder of the state to Fort Boise (after 1843). A few would strike out for California from Boise, but most who reached that point had Oregon in mind. The Indians, mountainmen, and missionaries had beaten a path, but by 1840 it was a well-defined road. Relations at the two posts owned by Hudson's Bay were cordial, and the forts often provided the goods, at a healthy price, which enabled the pioneers to reach their Oregon or California destination.

In 1843 the army commissioned John C. Frémont to map and survey the trail to Oregon. With Kit Carson and Thomas Fitzpatrick, both former trappers, as guides, the Frémont expedition made its way through southern Idaho, into Utah, back to the trail, and across the state. The debonair Frémont, with an aggressive wife, Jessie Benton Frémont, and a senator father-in-law, Thomas H. Benton, kept detailed impressionistic notes of his travels. His exploits were published almost immediately, and they convinced many potential pioneers that the journey was feasible and that a wagon trip was practical. Thousands of Americans trekked across the Oregon Trail during the next few years. By the time most wagon trains or horse caravans reached Idaho, it was late summer. The road was choked with dust, and the rain came infrequently. Although Fort Hall and Fort Boise offered welcome respite, they were not the promised land. Pioneer after pioneer, oxen after oxen, and wagon after wagon passed across southern Idaho, finding not the slightest temptation to stay.

While the nation of Texas was being annexed and the seeds of the Mexican War were beginning to sprout, the United States and Great Britain finally agreed on the 49th parallel as a boundary from the Rocky Mountains to the Puget Sound. One of the main reasons for agreement to the long-desired American border, was the settlement of Oregon by thousands of Americans. The Hudson's Bay Company eventually withdrew, and American soldiers replaced them at the Oregon Trail way stations. A few lonely trappers still meandered through the mountains and valleys, but for the most part, Idaho was Indian land. Jesuit missionaries were in the north, but they lived and worked with the Indian people. For fifty years, after Lewis and Clark, Americans had been involved in Idaho, and now it was part of the United States. Yet native Americans had survived the loss of beaver, antelope, and buffalo. Only the Mormons and gold could provide the permanent white settlers that would remove the Indian barrier.

3

God + Gold = Territory

IDAHO reflects much of the national pattern of western frontier settlement. Although tens of thousands of pioneers passed through the barren sagebrush of the Snake River valley, it was inevitable that some would decide to stay. Once again, Idaho's geographical divisions illustrate different reasons for settlement. In the southeast, Idaho was settled as an extension of Brigham Young's Mormon Empire. In the north and southwest, permanence came because of gold and other mineral discoveries. The two movements occurred almost simultaneously and led directly to the establishment of Idaho Territory and the initial subjugation of the native Americans. Much of the early settlement occurred during the divisive Civil War. In 1862, the United States Government opened most of the West for individual homestead ownership.

The Mormon experience in Idaho was planned and organized out of Salt Lake City. It was part of Brigham Young's grandiose scheme to establish communities and missions throughout the Rocky Mountains and even into California. As part of this plan, missions were organized for the purpose of Christianizing, baptizing, and pacifying the Indians. According to Mormon theology, the native Americans are a chosen people, one of the tribes of Israel, who deserve the blessings of Christianity. Realistically, Young was more interested in establishing Mormon control over as much land as possible and the conversion of native

Americans was of secondary importance. During the early 1850s, groups were sent to southern Utah, California, Nevada, and, in 1855, to Idaho. Twenty-seven men, led by Thomas S. Smith, made the 380-mile journey north into what was then Oregon Territory.

With eleven wagons and numerous animals, the expedition made its way to Fort Hall and then crossed to the northwest bank of the Snake River. It seems that the missionaries were unclear about their destination but decided to seek out converts in the Salmon River country. Where the Snake River turns south after skirting the Grand Tetons, Smith led his missionary following through the desert to the northwest. A Bannock chief met the Mormons and persuaded them to settle on the Lemhi River where they would have missionary access to the Shoshoni, Bannocks, Nez Percé, and Flatheads. Every summer the tribes met and traded in that area, and fished for the spawning salmon. They constructed a small fort only a few miles from where Meriwether Lewis first entered Idaho a half century earlier. One of their group described the location and construction of the fort:

> Our fort stands on the eastern bank of the Limhi [*sic*] River near a small stream coming in from the east. The fort is a timber stockade sixteen rods square and about twelve feet in height, with the buildings fifteen or twenty feet on the inside. All were made of wood and had a neat comfortable appearance.[1]

It was late in June before the missionaries diverted water onto about ten acres of land and planted corn, peas, potatoes, and turnips. Although the crops were well watered, an early September frost and grasshoppers made short work of the harvest. In fact, the insects were successful the next year in destroying the entire grain crop. Convinced that his party's supplies were inadequate to survive the winter, Smith sent two expeditions back to Salt Lake City during the first year. They returned with needed supplies and more colonists, including some of the missionaries' families. A sawmill, gristmill, and blacksmith shop

1. Lewis W. Shurtliff Journal, Nov. 19, 1855, in Merrill D. Beal and Merle W. Wells, *History of Idaho,* 3 vols. (New York: Lewis Historical Publishing Co., 1959), 1: 251–252.

were constructed, and as more acres were planted, Fort Lemhi took on the appearance of a permanent farming community, not just a mission. Filled with optimism, and impressed by the economic and strategic potential of Fort Hall, the Mormons sent three of their group across the Bitterroots into Montana in an unsuccessful attempt to purchase Fort Hall. This transformation of the settlement—from mission to village—was not lost on the native Americans.

Initially, harmony existed between the missionaries and the various groups of Indians. Over a hundred Indians were baptized by the Mormons and the religious aspect of the mission seemed to progress well. All of the missionaries were encouraged to learn an Indian language, preferably Shoshoni, and to instruct in the native tongue. A mission school was established to aid in this endeavor. As more reinforcements arrived, the missionaries planned to expand northward. In the spring of 1857, Brigham Young, accompanied by many of the leaders of the LDS church and a Ute chief, visited the mission. Young brought well over one hundred people with him and they surveyed the entire area for future growth and expansion. The church leader mildly chastised the missionaries for going too far away and expressed his opinion that the Snake River valley should have been settled first. In Young's mind, it appeared that settling permanently was paramount to converting Indians. The missionaries were also advised to marry young Indian girls to cement the friendship that already had developed.

After Young's visit, there was no doubt that Fort Lemhi was to become a permanent settlement. Heretofore all land had been worked co-operatively, but after the leader's departure, the mission was divided and the settlers drew lots for the land. A lower fort was built two miles south of Fort Lemhi. More reinforcements were sent from Utah, and the harvest of 1857 was adequate. By that fall, a mood of general satisfaction and optimism pervaded the colonists' attitudes. Irrigation had proved that crops would prosper in the high mountain valley, and the cordial relations with the various tribes appeared established. Little did the pioneers realize that they would not see spring in the Lemhi valley.

A number of forces led to the abandonment of the Salmon River Mission, but the two most prominent were the changed attitude of Idaho's Indians and the difficulties between the federal government and Utah Mormons. Ever since the California gold rush had diverted much of the western travel from the Oregon Trail to Salt Lake City, trouble had been brewing between Brigham Young and federal officials. Young, the territorial governor, used his religious and secular authority to circumvent the federal marshals and judges. On the other hand, the federal officials did all they could to paint a gloomy picture of conditions in Utah. The upshot was that President James Buchanan sent a new governor to Utah accompanied by an army under Albert Sidney Johnston authorized to quell the "Mormon rebellion." Brigham Young used guerrilla tactics to postpone the army's arrival. The knowledge of the approaching army and Young's resolve to fight had an effect on the Salmon River Mission.

Other Americans in the area, mountaineers and traders, both in Idaho and Montana, feared the expansion of Mormonism into their areas. Indeed, Indian agents reported that the Mormons were offering ammunition to the Indians in order to fight the federal army. Rumors and threats and fear circulated among Mormons and non-Mormons alike. At the center of their fears were the native Americans. Of course, the Indians were told that the Mormons were after their land, that Mormons only converted them to make them peaceful. The mountaineers also realized that Johnston's army needed supplies and persuaded the Indians to raid the Lemhi mission.

Some of the activities of the Mormons had already upset the Indians prior to the difficulty over the federal army. The construction of a second fort and the building of numerous fences were not ignored by the nomadic natives. The continual arrival of more reinforcements gave the mission the appearance of permanence, which did not set well with the Bannocks. Finally, the settlers had caught more salmon than they really needed and had exported eight wagonloads to Utah. This exploitation of a vitally needed resource caused ire among the Indians.

The ingredients of cultural clash were brought to a head during the 1857 Christmas season when the missionaries enter-

tained a band of Nez Percé, who then stole sixty head of Shoshoni horses. While at the fort, the Nez Percé had performed a
war dance, and to the Bannock and Shoshoni, it seemed that the
Mormons were harboring their enemy. Consequently, the other
tribes were upset over the continual cordial treatment afforded
the Nez Percé. At various times in January and February, the
Shoshonis or Bannocks came to the fort brandishing weapons or
demanding grain. A mountaineer trader, John W. Powell, who
lived with the Indians, warned the Mormons that an attack was
pending. However, Smith did not believe Powell, who had
never been friendly to the Mormons before, and who had been
telling the Indians where they could sell their stolen livestock.

In late February the Bannocks and Shoshonis attempted to
steal most of the cattle herd. The missionaries fought the Indians; two of the Mormons were killed and most of the cattle
were taken. In the dramatic attempt to prevent their herd from
being stolen, the missionaries were overwhelmed by the more
numerous Indians. As they retreated into the fort, it was decided
to send men to Salt Lake City immediately for counsel and support. The isolation of their situation had finally become evident.
However, there was no recurrence of the Indian warfare; in fact,
many of the Indians came back around the mission shortly after
the raid. Still, Brigham Young decided to abandon the mission
and bring the entire group back to Utah. He had already urged
the same course for other missions scattered throughout the
West. The army of Johnston was on its way and the LDS people
must be united. When the relief expedition arrived, the pioneers
were packed and ready to leave. Slightly less than three years
after they had openly moved into the Lemhi valley, the Mormons were in retreat. On departing, Thomas Smith gave nearly
a thousand bushels of wheat to the Shoshoni chief, Snagg, who
had converted to Mormonism. The Mormons had learned that
the land could be conquered and that given water, it would
produce. It had also been their misfortune to learn that the native Americans were not going to sit by and watch the white
colonization of their beloved homeland.

Prior to the founding of the Salmon River Mission at Fort
Lemhi, few whites would risk planting and harvesting in a

country deemed to be the stronghold of Indians. As far as the Mormons were concerned, the breakup of the Lemhi valley mission simply arrested the colonizing movement. The pressure for agricultural expansion continued, and as soon as the Utah-federal government differences were resolved, Mormons once again pushed northward. This time they were more conservative and only penetrated a few miles at a time. Success accompanied these more patiently organized efforts.

About two years after the Fort Lemhi missionaries returned to Utah, Thomas Smart led a handful of Mormons into northern Cache valley. Near a bluff overlooking the beautiful little Cub River, a tributary of the Bear, they founded Franklin, Idaho's first permanent white settlement. Although Brigham Young and Orson Pratt had surveyed the area and located the 42nd parallel, most of these land-thirsty pioneers did not realize that two miles south of their new homes they had crossed the invisible boundary and were actually in Washington Territory. It would be a few years before they were fully aware of the fact that they were not citizens of Utah. As more families arrived, a fort and a common corral were constructed and a communal irrigation ditch was completed. A sawmill, gristmill, and creamery soon provided many of the needs for the community. Franklin was so close to other Cache valley communities that the settlers did not worry about isolation and loneliness. It was occupation a small step at a time.

The Franklin pattern was copied as other border areas soon became outreaches of Mormonism. The remainder of Idaho's Cache valley, Bear Lake valley, and Malad valley were all settled by either pioneers seeking new land or those Brigham Young requested to pull up roots and go to a new area. By the time the Civil War ended and Idaho Territory was organized, southeastern Idaho was dotted with small, but permanent, agrarian communities. Many Scandinavian and English converts found their long-sought Zion in the valleys of southern Idaho.

Most of the pioneers realized immediately that the winters were more difficult than any they had experienced. The growing season was so short that the settlers were limited in what they could produce. Many of the Bear Lake pioneers left the valley after the winter of 1864–1865 simply because there was too much snow for too long a time. Another problem these pioneers faced was that they could be asked to pick up and move to another new settlement regardless of their success or failure in the first. Many of Idaho's earliest citizens were later sent into other Idaho valleys or to Wyoming, southern Utah, Arizona, or even Canada. They were part of an earthly kingdom that transcended homestead law, deeds, and titles.

Ultimately, the Mormon agrarian influence spread from far eastern Idaho, Bear Lake, and Teton Valley, to south central Idaho. Much of the upper Snake River valley was settled by nineteenth-century Mormon pioneers, as was south central Idaho. A considerable amount of their cultural baggage was transported into these remote areas instantly. Most Mormon towns soon had small weekly newspapers, and amateur theater was attempting to alleviate the depressions of winter. During the first winter in Bear Lake, the pioneers presented the play *William Tell*. Schools were founded, and, although the sessions were comparatively short, the fundamental subjects were taught with dedication and authority.

Another contribution of these adventuresome individuals was their development of irrigation techniques. One of Idaho's geographical features that frightened Oregon- or California-bound easterners was the apparent lack of trees and the abundance of sagebrush. It was obvious that water was lacking. At first, only the natural streams were diverted, but later came dams, reservoirs, and canals. Ditch or canal companies were organized, and each farmer was entitled to so many shares of water, meaning he could use the water for a designated period of time. It was the control and distribution of the vast water supply that enabled early pioneers to survive and even experience some prosperity. The key to the later development of much of Idaho's agricultural potential was water control, and the pioneer co-operative canal companies established precedents for future use.

While the early Mormon pioneers were beginning to cultivate Indian land and create communities in southern Idaho, people of an entirely different character were coming and going through-

out the rest of the state. Thousands of gold hunters were prospecting at a fantastic rate. Ever since the rush to California,
every stream in the West was a potential strike. The lure of gold
and the ever-present rumors of more gold or silver inevitably led
a mob into Idaho. The gold seekers went where the gold was
supposed to be regardless of international, national, or reservation boundaries. As usual, Idaho's Indians were caught in an
unwanted crossfire.

The heavy concentration of Indians and numerous strikes
elsewhere had kept the miners out of northern Idaho for many
years. However, after the Coeur d'Alenes were defeated near
Spokane, Washington, in 1858 and placed on a reservation, the
way was open for more exploration and exploitation of northern
Idaho. During 1858–1859 army Capt. John Mullan attempted to
construct a road from Fort Walla Walla to Fort Benton on the
upper Missouri River. It connected the steamboat landing on the
Missouri with routes down the lower Columbia. The route he
selected roughly corresponds with Interstate 10 today. Construction included cutting much heavy timber, excavating, and bridg-
ing the Coeur d'Alene River twenty times. While engaged in the
construction, one of Mullan's hunters found a handful of coarse
gold. Mullan, fearful of losing his crew to a gold rush, tried to
play the incident down; yet it would be only a matter of time
before prospectors were using the Mullan road to get to the
Idaho mineral resources, and John Mullan was trying to use his
knowledge of the area to become the first territorial governor.
After strikes were made in northeastern Washington and in British Columbia, many miners used Walla Walla, Washington, as
an outfitting point. Elias D. Pierce, a former prospector and Nez
Percé trader, decided that the time was ripe for a move into the
Clearwater area. The Nez Percé had not participated in the
Coeur d'Alene wars of the 1850s; yet they tightly controlled the
access to the Clearwater River and its tributaries. Any prospectors were going to have to confront Nez Percé authority and
treaty rights headon.

At the same time that Mormon pioneers were preparing to irrigate the soil around Franklin, and Abraham Lincoln was won-
dering how to provision the federal fort at Charleston, South

Carolina, E. D. Pierce and a group of ten prospectors were sneaking past Nez Percé sentinels onto the forks of the Clearwater. The Nez Percé knew that the discovery of gold would mean a mammoth intrusion into their lands, and their Indian agent, A. J. Cain, protested against the illegality of prospecting on the Nez Percé Reservation. Cain and the Nez Percé were soon to learn that treaties became meaningless when the discovery of gold was a possibility. It was eventually agreed that the miners could work north of the Clearwater, but not south. That agreement, like others, was short-lived.

Pierce succeeded in panning a substantial amount of gold out of Orofino Creek not too far from where Lewis and Clark had emerged from their ordeal in the Clearwater Mountains. He described the success in glowing terms and also explained how a mining district was established: "On the 1st of October commenced our labor. Found gold in every place in the stream—I never saw a party of men so much excited; they made the hills and mountains ring with shouts of joy." [2] The miners then set up the boundaries of their mining district, drafted a code of mining laws, and elected a recorder. A townsite was surveyed into building lots, and the miners agreed to call it Pierce City.

After considerable publicity in West Coast newspapers, the rush was on. Soon the individual pan was replaced by the sluice box or the rocker as thousands of prospectors hopefully and intently watched the heavy gold dust and fine sand separated from the rest of the gravel. The abundance of water was essential to successful gold mining operations, and Idaho was not found wanting. By the spring of 1861, Lewiston had become an outfitting and supply station. Reuben, a Nez Percé chief, built a warehouse in Lewiston and joined with an old mountainman, William Craig, who was married to a Nez Percé woman, in the operation of a ferry across the Snake and the Clearwater. The Washington territorial legislature created a county, Shoshone, and the population poured into the mining districts.

Once a rush was underway, those who were less successful would follow the freshest rumor into another area with reckless

2. E. D. Pierce, *Reminiscences,* Oct. 1, 1860, microfilm copy, Idaho State Library, Boise.

abandon. Contrary to the agreement with the Nez Percé, prospectors moved south of the Clearwater within a month. At Elk
City, fifty miles south and east of Pierce, they struck pay dirt.
Eventually a flume nine miles long was constructed to bring the
necessary water to the diggings. By the end of 1866, when
Pierce and Elk City had begun to return fewer dividends, it is
estimated that the two areas had yielded more than seven million dollars worth of gold. The final gleaning was done by the
frugal Chinese, who were able to do quite well in the mines,
even though they were severely discriminated against by Anglo
miners.

By the summer of 1861, prospectors had unearthed a particularly rich placer on Nez Percé land near the Salmon River at
Florence. Although the Nez Percé initially threatened the
invaders with expulsion, they finally relented and agreed to the
illegal intrusion. In fact, if the Indians had not been willing to
provide food and supplies, many of the miners would have
perished in the mountainous terrain. By the spring of 1862,
Florence had nearly five thousand people. Another strike a few
miles away at Warrens also yielded an abundance of gold. The
North Salmon diggings produced nearly sixteen million dollars
worth of gold by 1867. These were rich deposits, but the prosperity was at best temporary.

Although totally on Nez Percé land, Lewiston became the
supply headquarters for most of the north Idaho gold strikes. A
newspaper, the *Golden Age,* was published and numerous buildings were constructed there. It was also in Lewiston that the
Henry Plummer gang decided it was easier to rob miners than to
pan for gold. They harassed miners from Orofino to Walla
Walla. Finally some of the gang were exiled by Lewiston citizens. The road agents left for Florence and then Montana where
Plummer was eventually killed by vigilantes.

It is a sad fact of American history that while hundreds of
thousands of uniformed Americans in Virginia, Tennessee, and
Maryland were trying to kill each other, thousands of Americans in the West were running from creek to brook to river trying to get rich quickly. In Florence, Civil War passions were intense, and some people feared an outbreak of violence between

Union and Confederate empathizers. News of the war came into Idaho slowly, but was greeted by numerous deserters, draft-jumpers, and others with great interest.

At the very time Robert E. Lee was contemplating an invasion of the North in August 1862, Moses Splawn, who had been in Elk City and Florence the previous year, led a group of men into the Boise Basin. Splawn had been told by an Indian that there was definitely gold south of the Salmon. Joined by other prospectors led by George Grimes, they found gold and hostile Indians, who quickly drove them out of the mountains. That fall, reinforced by hundreds of gold-seeking adventurers, the prospectors moved back into the Boise Basin and struck it rich at Idaho City. Within a few years, the miners expanded to other towns such as Placerville, Rocky Bar, and Atlanta.

The Boise Basin rapidly became the most productive and populated part of Idaho. Some estimate that nearly sixteen thousand people summered in the basin during 1864. By then Idaho City had hundreds of buildings and a population in excess of six thousand. An interesting product of the basin bonanza was the development of the city of Boise a few miles away on the Boise River. A military detachment was assigned to the region to protect the miners from Indians who were being rambunctious in their activities along the wagon and freight trails. At the same time, many farmers decided to stay in the Boise area rather than push on to Oregon because money could be made by supplying the numerous mining towns and the troops at Fort Boise. Within a short time, Boise became a supply source for miners rushing into the basin or, later, to the Owyhee country south of Boise. By 1866, the Boise Basin strike produced more than twenty-four million dollars in gold. The topography and climate were not inhospitable, and the adjacent areas offered permanent settlers good agrarian opportunities. In that respect, the entire area differed from the goldfields in the northern mountains.

The development of Idaho City took place with interesting by-products. Although parts of the wooden city were burned four times by 1871, it had many of the cultural characteristics that accompanied frontier settlement. Every year saw different acting troupes finding their way to Idaho City for a season of entertainment. The theatrical productions, whether melodrama or Shakespeare, were a welcome relief for the hard-driving miners. The gambling halls were omnipresent, as were the famous dancing girls and the notorious madames.

Two famous Idaho ladies were Peg-Leg Annie Morrow and China Polly Bemis, who developed their talents in Idaho's goldfields. Annie Morrow had come to Atlanta, on the south side of the Sawtooths, in 1864. Orphaned, she married young to escape the lecherous advances of the numerous grizzled miners. After her husband was shot and three of her five children had died of diseases, she turned to the bottle and eventually to prostitution. Annie gained fame by attempting to cross the divide between Rocky Bar and Atlanta during a winter blizzard. Accompanied by a friend, Dutch Em, the two women became lost and were stranded in the mountains for three days. Exhausted, Em collapsed, so Annie gave her all her coats and underclothing, but the big German girl died. When a rescue party found Annie Morrow, she was wandering on hands and knees, covered only by a thin dress. The miners saved her life by amputating both of her feet with a hunting knife and meat saw. Henry Longheme, an Italian saloonkeeper, started a fund that provided artificial legs for Annie. She lived with Longheme for twenty-two years, but then he deserted her and returned to Italy with her life savings, estimated at more than ten thousand dollars. She lived well into the twentieth century and operated a rooming house-restaurant in Atlanta and Rocky Bar.

China Polly Bemis was one of the many Chinese prostitutes imported into the mining boom towns. She was a tiny slave-girl owned by a type of male overseer, Big Jim, who profited from the earnings of a group of prostitutes. China Polly was taken to Warrens in the Salmon River country and when her owner died, she refused to hire out to another man and instead opened a small restaurant. When Charly Bemis was shot on the porch of her restaurant, she nursed him back to health and then went with him to his diggings on Bemis Point, a few miles east of Riggins on the Salmon. Twenty years later, she became his legal wife. She spent over sixty years on the Salmon River and became a legend of the mining days.

A Boise newspaper editor described some of the mining camp girls in a scathing editorial: "Ye pining, lolling, screwed-up, wasp-waisted, putty-faced, consumption-mortgaged and novel-devouring daughters of fashion and idleness, you are no more fit for matrimony than a pullet is to look after a family of fifteen chickens." [3] Since the women were few and the winters were long, it is doubtful that the prospectors cared much about looks. It is noted that when a wagonload of young ladies arrived in one camp simultaneously with a load of watermelons, one chivalrous young miner paid eight dollars for a melon to give to the girls.

Most of Idaho's gold boom towns faded rapidly because of the terrain. Communities like Warrens and Florence were lost in the mountainous valleys that dominate most of the state. When pack trails provided the only access in and out of a mining camp, few, other than miners, braved the journey. Soon, the action shifted from Lewiston and the northwest to Boise because Boise could be supplied overland from California and by freighters out of Salt Lake City. Of course, as the placers played out, the population dwindled as well. Idaho may have had as many as twenty-four thousand people in 1864, but the census of 1870 revealed only fifteen thousand. Miners were mobile and nomadic and few had any long-term investment in the territory they prospected.

An interesting aspect of Idaho gold mining is that by 1870 over one-half of Idaho's miners and nearly one-third of the territory's population were Chinese. The Orientals purchased claims from the less-patient whites and worked them long after the original owners had left. Although Chinese miners and prostitutes had to pay extra taxes in many towns, they were able to make a living in the Idaho mines. Racial animosity grew, and in 1866 and 1867, massacres occurred in which over a hundred Orientals were killed. Naturally, these lynchings were usually blamed on the Indians. Individual and collective frustrations were often taken out on the Chinese minority. It seemed that the Orientals devised a method of mixing gold with certain other

3. Taken from Fashion Exhibit, Idaho State Museum, Boise. On display August 1975.

alloys that enhanced the weight. When this trickery was discovered, it also led to retribution. Nevertheless, the Chinese were a significant element of Idaho's golden era. The pursuit of sudden riches knew no racial or sexual bounds. It was a bizarre period, and the individuals who roamed the hills of Idaho were a strange collection of characters. Few made it big; it would take investors, trusts, corporations, plus the development of shafts and the payment of hourly wages, to bring most of the mineral wealth to the surface. By then, the individual miner had become just another tiny gear in a gigantic industrial machine.

Idaho's native Americans had witnessed the miners' exploitation of the rivers and creeks, timber, and wildlife. When the gold seekers left, the miners were not concerned about the environment they had disrupted and in some cases destroyed. In a few short years—the years of the Civil War plus one—they had taken more than fifty million dollars worth of gold from the mountains of Idaho Territory. But the miners usually left, and the Indians once again controlled the devastated diggings. More ominous to the future for Idaho's Indians were the farming settlers who had come to stay. These white men diverted streams and plowed the land and built fences.

Although the orderly and organized settlement of southeastern Idaho by Mormons brought a stable agrarian population into the area north of the 42nd parallel, it was the disorganized and chaotic surge to the goldfields of the north and southwest that brought government into Idaho. Ironically, government for Idaho came about by political disputes in Washington Territory more than by the desires of the diversified Idaho citizenry.

For whatever reasons, the Civil War Congress busily engaged in state and territorial creation throughout the Civil War. Much of the action taken was based on pure politics. Congress wanted to make sure that the West was more strongly cemented to the Union and did what it could to provide Republican party mortar. In many cases, representatives and senators knew very little about the geographical regions they were creating but listened to lobbyists from the territory who claimed to have all of the answers—at least the answers that would best serve the lobbyists' interests. Such was the case with the manipulations that led to the development of Idaho Territory in 1863. The natural geographical boundaries were ignored and artificial lines evolved.

The year before Franklin and Pierce were founded, Oregon's eastern boundary had been fixed when the area was granted statehood. All of Idaho was part of Washington Territory when the settlers and the miners moved into the area. Upon reading descriptions of the land between Nebraska and Oregon, senators and congressmen concluded that it would be a long time before they had to deal directly with that massive area of rivers, forests, and deserts.

As thousands of miners moved into northern Idaho, local politicians attempted to solve the future of Washington Territory. They were probably ignorant of their constituents in Cache valley, but the Mormons in Franklin did not fully realize where they were anyway. Three Washington politicians, each of whom were attempting to become Washington Territory's congressman, all privately agreed that they would work for a separation of the northern mining districts into a new territory. That idea would have been fine if Olympia, Vancouver, and Walla Walla—all Washington communities—had not been engaged in a mini-civil war to see which was going to be the capital of the territory. Originally, Olympia favored a reorganization of Washington that would move the eastern boundary from the western border of the Dakotas to the Cascades. This change would make Washington smaller, but would keep Olympia the capital. Vancouver on its part simply wanted the capital shifted there because of its location on the Columbia River, and Walla Walla felt that its location in the center of the territory should give it the prominent position. When miners rushed into Florence in 1862 and the Clearwater mines continued to grow, the situation became more confused. Lewiston surpassed Walla Walla in population and citizens of the former began to talk of being the capital of Washington Territory. The eastern mining districts sent representatives to Olympia, and they were opposed to territorial division. They wanted Washington to remain large, but with eastern control, preferably in Lewiston. In the meantime, Olympia proposed a new plan that would extend the eastern border of Oregon northward and thus create a well-defined and Olympia-controlled Washington. Since the legislature could not agree on any proposal, it was left for Congress to solve the local dispute.

When Congress met in late 1862, the lawmakers were faced with four possible solutions to the dilemma. It is well to remember that 1862 was a bad year for the Union troops, and decisions concerning territories in the Northwest had to be a low-priority problem. A simple solution for Congress would have been to declare the Cascade Mountains the eastern boundary of Washington and to create a new territory that would encompass the entire Columbia Basin north and east of Oregon. Another option was to retract Washington's eastern boundary to the Columbia River. But Congress never considered these two options very seriously. It decided to choose between Olympia's final proposal, a line north from Lewiston, and Walla Walla's proposed solution, a line eastward extending the Oregon-Washington boundary to the continental divide in present-day Montana. This last plan would have made Washington a gigantic state with Walla Walla planted right in the middle. The new creation would have taken in Florence as well as the new mines in the Boise Basin. John Mullan, the roadbuilder, had gone east to represent Walla Walla's interests and had proved quite persuasive. This territory would include a portion of Dakota Territory, Montana's Bitterroot valley, and the mines of Montana. It was this proposal that was adopted by the House of Representatives in February 1863.

When the bill was sent to the Senate, the lobbyists representing Olympia's interests were favored with timing and good luck. Washington's congressional delegate, William H. Wallace, a personal friend of Lincoln, worked with others to convince the Senate that Washington needed to be pared down. There was little concern for the size of the new territory. What Wallace was interested in was getting the eastern border of Washington established directly north from Lewiston. This plan succeeded and passed the Senate. The new territory included all of present-day Idaho and Montana, and, because the area of Nebraska was being condensed in preparation for statehood, nearly all of Wyoming. Even the choice of the name, *Idaho,* lacked dramatic inspiration. *Shoshone* and *Montana* were also suggested as names, but Massachusetts Sen. Henry Wilson, who had got Colorado's name changed from *Idaho,* decided the time had come to use the word for a territory. In size, the original Idaho was a geographic monstrosity larger than Texas. The House passed the bill on the final day of the session of Congress. The Walla Walla people wailed and screamed about the haste, but Lincoln signed the Idaho Organic Act into law the next day, March 4, 1863. William Wallace was appointed governor the following week, and the politics of territory-making were over for a year.

An act of Congress may create a paper territory, but for months the people of Walla Walla and Lewiston were not quite sure of their status. Indeed, Idaho's first years as a territory were a kind of cruel national joke. Finally, Wallace arrived in Lewiston in mid-July 1863 and set about establishing a government. Lewiston was the center of a government that included the Montana mines, the Mormon area of southeastern Idaho, and Fort Laramie in eastern Wyoming, which was nearly a thousand miles from Lewiston by any route. The selection of Lewiston as capital was also illegal. The town was on Nez Percé land and, according to the 1855 treaty, could not be involved in another territory's governing. This problem was remedied by a new treaty, which further reduced the Nez Percé Reservation by removing Lewiston and other adjacent areas. Although the Lapwai Nez Percé signed this treaty, the Nez Percé in Oregon did not. This new treaty, in effect, was one of the causes of the Nez Percé War a decade later. The entire territory allegedly had more than thirty thousand inhabitants, but that could change with the next gold strike. Wallace appointed territorial officials and then immediately began campaigning to become Idaho's congressional delegate. Although Wallace won the seat, his victory was tarnished when one of his supporters, collecting the returns, reported more than four hundred Wallace votes out of Fort Laramie when the population of the fort was only one hundred.

It was obvious to most officials that this gigantic territory required further surgery. One example of the problems presented by its size was the difficulty faced by the delegates from the Montana mines in retracing their journey home after the territorial legislature adjourned in February 1864. They left Lewiston and went down the river to Portland, then south to San Francisco. At San Francisco they turned east and traveled overland more than seven hundred miles to Salt Lake City, then they turned north and returned to the mining area. Although their homes were only about three hundred miles from Lewiston, the harsh winter conditions forced them to spend several months traveling about two thousand miles. Of course, they may have enjoyed certain aspects of Portland and San Francisco that were yet unavailable in Virginia City.

Another problem surfaced during the winter of 1863–1864. Neither territorial nor county government had begun to function in the eastern region of Montana, and when a spirit of lawlessness and violence swept the Montana mines, the Idaho officials were helpless. There was no way they could get to the area in time to restore peace, so vigilante justice took over, justice so often noted for its lack of justice. Although the legislature organized counties for the entire territory, it was apparent that a new territory was needed and could be justified.

Once again William Wallace led the battle in the halls of Congress. While various congressional committees were beginning to discuss forms of Reconstruction and others were investigating the conduct of the Civil War, Wallace went to work with other lobbyists to divide the infant Idaho Territory. Their most controversial proposal—one despised in northern Idaho—was the establishment of the Montana-Idaho boundary at the Bitterroots rather than at the continental divide. The residents of Lewiston hoped for an increased area of influence, but when Congress adopted the Bitterroot line, the narrow Panhandle was created. It is squashed between Washington and Montana, and natural boundaries are totally ignored. Montana came into existence in May of 1864, much of Wyoming was attached to the Dakota Territory, and the future influence of Lewiston, although the seat of territorial government, was in question.

During the first territorial legislative session, the delegates from the Boise Basin and those from Virginia City, Montana, combined to recommend that the permanent capital be established in Boise, which by 1864 was the population center. The northern Idaho delegates denounced this liaison as a corrupt bargain and the proposal died with adjournment. It did not die, however, outside the legislative halls. What could not be done by legislation, could be accomplished by deceit, subterfuge, and pure comedy.

Abraham Lincoln sent Caleb Lyon from New York to become the new territorial governor. Lyon, an egotist of the highest order, found the government in chaos when he finally arrived in Lewiston. The previous administration had gained notoriety for the corrupt ballot-stuffing from Laramie and the acting governor, William Daniels, had tried to collect wages as both territorial secretary and governor. Inhabitants of northern Idaho still wanted a new territory created for themselves out of eastern Washington and western Montana. Since southern Idaho outnumbered the northern section by at least eight to one, the Boise delegates voted a capital relocation bill through the legislature, and Boise was chosen to replace Lewiston as the capital. After Lyon signed the bill, the Lewiston partisans resorted to the local courts and obtained an injunction against the removal of the capital.

Meanwhile, Caleb Lyon could not cope with such western shenanigans. With some supporters, he devised a plan to take the government to Boise. He waited until after Christmas 1864, and then went, ostensibly, to hunt ducks on the Snake River. After he had hiked about six miles, two southern Idaho legislators helped him board a carriage, and the governor of Idaho escaped from his executive jurisdiction and went to Walla Walla. Lyon then plotted to steal the territorial seal and archives, but the Lewiston natives put the documents under a six-man, twenty-four-hour armed guard. With most of the territorial officials gone, Lewiston's citizens once again appealed to Congress to create a new northern territory and proposed to let southern Idaho go to the devil.

While Idaho government drifted aimlessly, the pompous Lyon went to Portland and began a lecture series on his world

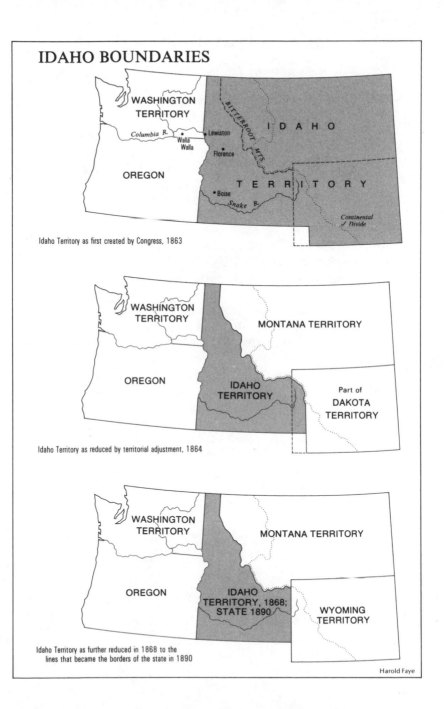

IDAHO BOUNDARIES

WASHINGTON TERRITORY

Columbia R.

Walla Walla

Lewiston

Florence

OREGON

Boise

Snake R.

I D A H O

T E R R I T O R Y

BITTERROOT MTS.

Continental Divide

Idaho Territory as first created by Congress, 1863

WASHINGTON TERRITORY

MONTANA TERRITORY

OREGON

IDAHO TERRITORY

Part of DAKOTA TERRITORY

Idaho Territory as reduced by territorial adjustment, 1864

WASHINGTON TERRITORY

MONTANA TERRITORY

OREGON

IDAHO TERRITORY, 1868; STATE 1890

WYOMING TERRITORY

Idaho Territory as further reduced in 1868 to the
lines that became the borders of the state in 1890

Harold Faye

travels. A solution to the fracas came with the arrival of a new territorial secretary, C. DeWitt Smith. Smith met Lyon in Portland, and then decided to go to Lewiston and steal the archives and seal. Smith also obtained an order for military assistance if needed. For a month, he played the role of pacifier in and around Lewiston. He carefully cultivated some accomplices and daily took a horseback ride for his health. While those guarding the territorial documents believed he was riding, Smith loaded the seal and archives on a boat, floated down the river, and left Lewiston for good. On April 14, 1865, Smith showed up in Boise with as many of the territorial records as he could carry. That same day, Abraham Lincoln was assassinated in Washington, D.C., and the new president, Andrew Johnson, reappointed Caleb Lyon to the governorship. The future seemed bleak for the new territory.

In the ten years since the Salmon River missionaries had attempted colonization, Idaho had become a territorial reality. Born of dubious midwifery in the midst of the Civil War, its original settlers had no use for boundaries or borders. Those in the southeast thought they were in Utah and acted as though that were so even after they found out the truth. Those in the north kept agitating for a separate existence and only participated with the others as a last resort. The Mormons went where they were told to go, and the prospectors went where they could go. Once the population was there, it was left for the politicians to create the government and the area to be governed. In the case of Idaho, they violated logic and nature and created from Indian lands inexplicable boundaries. It was natural that as more whites came and as new reservation treaties and restrictions were imposed, Idaho's native Americans would attempt to rid their land of the exploiting Anglos.

4

The Clash of Red and White

*T*HE contemporary traveler rarely views a fence as a symbol of confinement and estrangement. Few things the Anglo pioneers did were as alien to native American culture as the construction of fences. Although individual tribes inhabited specified areas, the idea of fences was incomprehensible. With the fence, the words "mine" and "yours" were applied to Mother Earth. To place poles around the earth and posts in it, and declare the ground owned by an individual, meant that others were denied access. The same was true of a mining claim. With a signature on a piece of paper, land that previously belonged to all was no longer universally available.

The Indians of Idaho were caught in the surge of the westward movement during the decade following the Civil War. Numerous red and white confrontations occurred because of the conflicting values and views of the land. Although referred to as wars, most battles were singular, rarely involved a massive deployment of warriors, and usually ended the particular dispute. Idaho's history of Indian difficulties culminated in the late 1870s and concluded with the reservation confinement of all major tribes.

The confrontations were the consequence of decades of interaction between opportunistic white pioneers or miners and the natives who finally resolved to resist further aggression. Idaho is no different than many other states in this regard, and the military resolution of Indian-white relations in Idaho is only a small chapter of a saga that began when the English, French, and Spanish first explored the continent. What is obvious is that the federal government, its representatives, and the white settlers continually moved onto land previously denied them by treaty or might. Indian retaliation came, and retaliation was followed by federal troops and more treaty negotiations. It was a cycle repeated often, with local variations of the main theme. Between 1850 and 1880, the Coeur d'Alenes, Bannocks, Shoshoni, northern Paiute, and Nez Percé acted out their version of the drama with tragic and demeaning results.

After the Whitman Massacre in 1849, there were a number of running battles in the Northwest. Many Idaho Indians participated in the Cayuse and the Yakima wars, although the actual battles were fought outside the current boundaries of Idaho. In 1858, the combined Palouse, Coeur d'Alenes, Spokanes, and Yakimas defeated the federal forces under Col. Edward J. Steptoe, a few miles west of the present Idaho border near Rosalia, Washington. Of course, it was all Washington Territory then. Col. George Wright was sent into the area, and, near Spokane, the army troops routed the Indians and forced a retreat. Wright was able to subdue the Coeur d'Alenes on the eve of the Civil War, and they were placed on a small reservation near the beautiful lakes and rivers of the Panhandle.

At the same time, Bannocks and Shoshonis in southern Idaho were becoming more aggressive in their attacks on emigrant and freight trains. Numerous trails and wagon roads cut across their traditional lands. The Bannocks and Shoshonis could not retreat very far or they would be encroaching on the territory claimed by the Utes, Paiutes, Flatheads, Crows, or Blackfeet. As the Lemhi mission experience illustrated, permanent settlers were beginning to penetrate deeper into the mountain valleys, and the Indians used force to evict these intruders when their presence became obnoxious to them. The Mormons, who adopted a policy of "better to feed than to fight," established compatible Indian-white relations in most areas of southeastern Idaho; yet, they carefully constructed forts around their villages.

A constant irritant to Indians was the fact that many fear-struck or hot-headed emigrants would shoot friendly Indians without provocation. The presence of federal troops who were accused of indiscriminately murdering or beating Indians also fanned the flames of Indian pride. The settlers, the emigrants, and the troops provided enough fuel, but when the Indians on their part added horse stealing and constant threats, southern Idaho was set ablaze for nearly three years. Throughout 1859 and 1860, every wagon train was liable to be attacked by marauding Bannocks or Shoshonis. They stole cattle, horses, and money, and would kill to obtain them. A further problem during this period was the tragic fact that many federal officials were accusing Mormons of inciting Indians to do violence against the emigrants, while the Mormons, who had abandoned Fort Lemhi, accused the federal troops of inciting the Indians to attack the mission. In both cases, the accusers claimed that the reward for violence was a ready market for the stolen livestock.

The small army detachments had the impossible task of patrolling hundreds of miles of wagon roads at a time when thousands of emigrants were moving West. It was not uncommon for a military officer to report seeing in excess of three hundred wagons in a single day and one group had "at least 7,000 head" of livestock. As that many animals and people cut a swath through Indian land, they devastated the environment upon which the native Americans received sustenance. Successive wagon trains had to graze their livestock farther away from the trail in order to obtain adequate feed. Since the wagon trails and the Indian trails were often the same, Indian travelers were also faced with the annoying problem of no grass. The buffalo and antelope had left the Snake River Plain, so emigrant livestock were viewed by the Indian as a potential substitute.

Another interesting point concerning Idaho's Bannocks and Shoshonis is that the federal government had no clear policy defining federal jurisdiction. The homeland of these people extended all across northern Utah. The Nevada, Oregon, and Montana agents quibbled about whether or not the Bannock and Shoshoni were in their jurisdiction. When they were finally placed under Indian Agent John Owen, in Montana, he could never obtain the promised federal annuity items, which should have provided some food and clothing. This situation made it fruitless to try to negotiate treaties that would keep the Indians away from the trails. So, the native Americans followed the pattern of life that had gradually evolved. They searched for food, stole horses, and attacked wagon trains to achieve the needed food and horses. Wagon trains, pony express riders, and freighters offered an easy road to success. However, reports of Indian conditions during the winter months found destitution, starvation, freezing, and continual suffering.

During the summer of 1861 and 1862, there were numerous reports of attacks along the Oregon and California trails. These incidents occurred all across the state, from the Boise valley on the west, beyond Massacre Rocks near American Falls, to Soda Springs in the east. The City of Rocks area of south central Idaho, on the California Trail, reported numerous attacks. Still, the emigrants rushed on and additional fuel was poured into the tinderbox when gold was discovered in the Boise Basin and in Montana. The Indian attacks became intense during the summer and early autumn of 1862, so that many people abandoned the California Trail route completely and veered southward to the Mormon settlements along the Bear River. The bold Indians followed them and began attacking farms and settlements in northern Utah. By now, the nation was in the midst of the Civil War, and federal troop protection was only a wishful thought.

At this point, Col. Patrick Edward Connor and his California Volunteers were dispatched from California to Utah to protect the wagon train routes and settlers from the Indians. Although the troops expressed a preference for fighting in Virginia, they soon became involved in a struggle of great significance to Idaho's Bannocks and Shoshoni. On his way to Utah, if Connor heard of an atrocity or even thievery, he would dispatch Maj. Edward McGarry to the scene. McGarry sent out scouting parties to pick up Indians abandoned by the main tribe, or others who just happened to be in the area. Then he would demand the surrender of Indians accused of an attack or a kidnapping or thievery within a certain time period. If the accused were not handed over, the hostages would be executed. Usually McGarry's troops did a great deal of executing, and, if the prisoners attempted escape, they were shot down. These executions inflamed the Shoshoni leaders, especially in December of 1862 when four Shoshonis were captured in the Bear River valley on the Utah-Idaho border and executed after another group had stolen some livestock.

Embittered, the Shoshoni met at Bear Lake and swore vengeance upon the whites. They announced that any white who crossed to the north side of the Bear River would be killed. They moved their main encampment into Cache valley and gathered on the north side of the river in Idaho. The Bannock allies of the Shoshoni had left for Montana, but even without the Bannocks, nearly six hundred Indians were ready to attack any white who ventured across the Bear.

After two express riders and a member of a freighting outfit were killed, Colonel Connor decided to move against the Shoshoni encampment. Under cover of night, he ultimately moved a force of three hundred men into Cache valley during January of 1863. The Shoshoni were well aware of the impending battle. Chief Bear Hunter had seen the troops coming while he was extorting wheat from the settlers in Franklin. Colonel Connor moved into Franklin, where his soldiers warmed themselves in the homes of settlers. Winter campaigns in the mountains were hard. Many of the soldiers were frostbitten and longed for a night's sleep in a real house. Fearing that the Shoshoni would escape, Connor rousted his men in the middle of a cold night and marched them nearly ten miles to a point across the river from the Shoshoni village. At daybreak he could see that the Shoshoni intended to fight. The Indians had chosen a deep ravine as their battleline, and it was a strong position. Depending on how the battle developed, the women and children could escape up the ravine into the foothills or down the ravine to the river. The Battle of Bear River was about to begin.

While Connor's infantry came directly toward the ravine in a frontal assault, cavalry units flanked the ravine at both ends, and the gully became a corridor of death. Fired by success, the California troopers turned the battle into a massacre as women and children were shot indiscriminately. The next day local settlers counted the dead and reported that nearly four hundred Shoshonis, including Bear Hunter, had died. Only twenty-two of the soldiers were killed in the four-hour conflict. A few wounded Indian children and women were taken into Mormon villages, but most of those who survived had escaped during the heat of the battle.

Connor's destruction of the Shoshonis drove the Indians away from the settlements and wagon trails, temporarily. Later in the spring, Connor, now a brigadier general, marched his troops to Fort Hall but could not locate the remaining Shoshonis. The Indians returned to their practice of attacking wagon trains and isolated way-stations. However, by the end of 1863, Connor was able to conclude three treaties with various groups of the Shoshoni. Indian Agent James Doty wrote to the commissioner of Indian affairs and aptly surveyed the reasons for the hostilities that led to the Battle of Bear River. Doty cited the scarcity of game and the occupation by whites of fertile ground as the driving forces behind Indian attacks. Reduced to a state of destitution, the Shoshoni and Bannock were compelled to plunder in order to survive. One Doty sentence is a classic understatement, yet it typifies the nation's Indian-white relationships: "It is not expected that wild and warlike people will tamely submit to the occupation of their country by another race, and to starvation as a consequence thereof." [1]

After nearly a decade of discussions and negotiations, the Shoshoni of southern Idaho agreed to move to the Fort Hall Reservation. In June 1867, President Andrew Johnson set aside nearly two million acres for the Shoshoni. The next year, the government tried to move the Fort Hall Shoshoni and the Bannock to the eastern Shoshoni reservation at Wind River, Wyoming. The Fort Hall Indians resisted this attempt and arranged to stay in Idaho—their traditional base. Both groups were allowed traditional privileges of root gathering and buffalo hunting, while the federal government was supposed to provide summer sustenance. Chief Tendoy's small band of Lemhis, who were mostly Shoshoni, refused to come to Fort Hall, and they

1. U.S. Office of Indian Affairs, *Annual Report of the Commissioner of Indian Affairs, 1863* (Washington, D.C.: Government Printing Office, 1864): 155.

were granted a reservation along the Lemhi River. In 1907, the Lemhis were incorporated into the Fort Hall complex.

Between 1866 and 1868, during the midst of the bitter feuds over national Reconstruction, western Shoshonis and northern Paiutes decided to drive intruding white miners out of southwestern Idaho. In what came to be called the Snake War, the Indians were able to disrupt mail and freight service to the mines as well as to harass farmers, armed volunteers, and the regular army. At a time when Idaho's territorial government was in total chaos because of Reconstruction, financing, and Indian problems, and almost everyone was trying to oust the governor, David W. Ballard—some even wanted to hang him—Gen. George Crook finally concluded a treaty to end the hostilities. After rounding up dissident Indians, under Eagle Eye, and convincing Chief Winnemucca's Paiutes to put away their weapons, Crook began negotiating the series of treaties that ultimately led to the formation of the Idaho-Nevada Duck Valley Reservation as well as others in Nevada and Oregon. The Snake War never reached the total proportions of other battles, but again it was an inevitable attempt by the Indians of southwestern Idaho to preserve their landed heritage.

One impropriety for which Governor Ballard was accused was his handling of the federal treaty funds sent to the Nez Percé Indians at their Lapwai Reservation. The payments were four years behind schedule, and the Nez Percé were becoming increasingly concerned about broken treaties and broken promises. Few occurrences in Idaho history have gained more notoriety than the so-called Nez Percé War of 1877. The subject of numerous biographies and a television documentary, young Chief Joseph, only thirty-seven years old, has become a romantic figure as the "Red Napoleon." In many respects, Joseph is deserving of the accolades, but in reality the Nez Percé removal and Joseph provide a historical reminder of the tragic drama of how the native Americans were pushed aside when they stood in the way of what whites deemed progress. Considering the Indian respect for nature and its bounties and their devotion to the land, the farmer's plow, the miner's pick, and the lumberman's axe were devastating to them. The forced evacuation from the environment and locale they loved is the tragedy of Joseph and the Nez Percé.

Ever since their initial contact with Lewis and Clark, the Nez Percé had maintained a positive attitude toward whites. Always insisting on their rights, they had signed an 1855 treaty which gave them the area between the Salmon and Clearwater rivers and in their beautiful ancestral Wallowa and Imnaha valleys in eastern Oregon. Old Joseph, Chief Joseph's father, understood that this domain was never to be invaded, and the Nez Percé treated these valleys as their homeland. The Nez Percé were quite successful in providing life's necessities in the beautiful mountains and valleys.

In 1863, when gold was discovered on the Clearwater River, many of the Nez Percé chiefs signed a treaty reducing the size of the Lapwai Reservation in Idaho, but the treaty stated also that Lapwai was the reservation for all Nez Percé. Old Joseph and the Nez Percé in Oregon did not sign the treaty nor did they move across the Snake. Oregon settlers and land developers could not keep their eyes off the land in eastern Oregon. The pressure intensified to such a point that before Old Joseph died, he extracted a promise from his son that he would never give up Wallowa. The Nez Percé were becoming aware of the long history of broken Indian-white treaties. As it had happened so many times before, the inevitable came in 1876. A federal commission yielded to the demands for Nez Percé removal and declared that all Nez Percé must go to the Lapwai Reservation whether they signed the 1863 treaty or not. Gen. O. O. Howard of the U.S. Army was ordered to enforce the decree.

Joseph, deeply distressed, requested discussions and conferences. Using reason and the treaties, he attempted to demonstrate that the Wallowa was the land of the Nez Percé forever. His efforts were futile, frustrating, and discouraging. The military and the commission would not reconsider; Joseph had until June 14, 1877, to move all of his people onto the Lapwai Reservation. The Nez Percé had thirty days to gather all of their belongings, cross the Hells Canyon of the Snake River, traverse rugged mountains, and arrive at a place already occupied by other Nez Percé. To compound their agony, it was spring in the

Wallowa and to leave their homeland during its most beautiful season embittered them.

Joseph realized that with Howard's army at his back, his only option was to migrate to the reservation. At this point, Joseph's painful conclusion was to go to Lapwai and leave Wallowa. He had decided against going to war. Joseph's concern was only to save his people as they sought to escape from the army. Other Nez Percé chiefs, Whitebird and Looking Glass, both with large followings, did not submit to the white intrusion. Slowly the Nez Percé, who numbered approximately seven hundred, moved from Oregon into Idaho. A small group of young Nez Percé men, infuriated by their situation, killed four whites in the Salmon River valley. Another band of Nez Percé accounted for at least fourteen more white deaths. When Howard received word of these attacks, he dispatched nearly one hundred cavalry under Capt. David Perry into Whitebird's canyon to punish the Nez Percé. Quickly deploying their warriors in three different strategic locations, the Nez Percé leaders sent a small delegation under a truce flag toward the soldiers. When the scouts saw the approaching Indians, they opened fire on the flag-bearing delegation. The concealed Nez Percé answered the fire, and when the battle ended, thirty-four U. S. cavalrymen were dead, while the Nez Percé counted only two wounded braves.

It is interesting to note that although the Nez Percé had defeated their immediate pursuers, they did not counter-attack against the survivors, nor did they retaliate against white settlers in the vicinity. Wishing to avoid further confrontations, they crossed the Salmon River and continued to elude the main force under Howard. There were many minor skirmishes between local volunteers who joined Howard and Nez Percé bands, but for the most part Joseph and the other chiefs were successful in keeping the women and children away from the army. When a couple of army scouting parties were virtually wiped out by the Nez Percé, Howard concluded that he was involved in a full military engagement and that it would be necessary to use all of the power he could muster. For the Nez Percé who were trying to avoid a war by going to a reservation, the issue was becoming increasingly clear. It would be impossible to go to the Lapwai Reservation, so they decided to follow their traditional hunting course across the Bitterroots to Montana.

Howard, who had nearly six hundred regulars at his command, caught the Nez Percé on the banks of the Clearwater and ordered a fullscale attack. But the battle ended in a draw. Joseph now led the entire band over the Lolo Trail, as if they were on their buffalo hunting expedition to Montana, except that all of the women and children, with all of their possessions, were part of the entourage. This was not a retreat; Howard and his army were too far behind to cause much concern. The Nez Percé believed they could join the Crows with little difficulty and settle with them. Joseph completely misunderstood that the entire Western Department of the United States Army was out to get him and his followers.

After crossing the Bitterroots, Joseph found his path blocked by an army detachment from Fort Missoula. The Nez Percé could have easily overwhelmed the troops who demanded surrender, but Joseph parlayed until his people had simply outflanked the army, and escaped up the Bitterroot valley. Although living off the land, the Nez Percé did not cut a destructive swath through the white settlements. It seems that they were making a concerted effort to avoid future antagonisms and hostilities. In their minds, their troubles were with General Howard, and they had left him struggling through the mountains of Idaho.

It was sad that the Nez Percé did not know the nature of their true enemy. On August 9, 1877, in western Montana's beautiful Big Hole Basin, Gen. John Gibbon led 180 soldiers and some civilians in a surprise attack on the Nez Percé encampment. The Nez Percé were so convinced that they were safe from Howard that they had failed to post guards or maintain scouts. Still, after the initial shock, the Nez Percé stiffened their resistance and successfully thwarted Gibbon's assault. Gibbon's forces lost twenty-nine dead, and would have suffered more if Howard had not arrived to reinforce the original attackers. When the Nez Percé retreated from the battlefield, they left behind eighty-three dead. More than fifty of those who perished were women and children. For a chief dedicated to saving his nation, it was a sad day for Joseph to leave the bodies of the innocent children and their mothers.

With braves entrenched in rifle pits to protect the rear guard, Joseph led the Nez Percé out of Big Hole across Horse Prairie and into the Lemhi valley of Idaho. Although some of the warriors took vengeance on local settlers, for the most part, the Nez Percé left the whites alone. They could have easily destroyed numerous farms and a small stockade at Junction, but chose to leave peaceably. A small band attacked some freighters at Birch Creek and killed five people. When informed of the Nez Percé location and direction of movement, Howard re-entered Idaho through Monida Pass and camped at Camas Meadows, only a few miles from the Indian camping grounds. During the night, about thirty Nez Percé sneaked into Howard's camp and drove off more than two hundred pack mules and forty horses before they were discovered. This tactic delayed Howard for a week, and once again the Nez Percé escaped. They left Idaho via spectacular Targhee Pass, crossed the continental divide, and passed through Yellowstone National Park. Howard, augmented by fifty Bannocks under Buffalo Horn, once again pursued the weary Nez Percé.

Easily outdistancing Howard, the Nez Percé made their way north toward Canada. Once again, they did not realize that another military force under Gen. Nelson A. Miles was moving in from the east to intercept them. Joseph and the other chiefs slowed their pace. The Nez Percé may have thought that they had already reached Canada when they camped near the Bear Paw Mountains around the first of October 1877. The more plausible reasons for the slowdown were the exhaustion of the people and the knowledge that Howard was far behind. The tragedy is that the delay allowed Miles to arrive at the Bear Paws and begin the assault that ended the flight. In the final siege and encounter, the Nez Percé feelings became clear. For the warriors and their families who wanted to go to Canada left, and Miles could not stop them. Joseph chose to remain with the majority of the tribe, and after five days of siege, Joseph, with head bowed in dignified solemnity, rode to the army camp and delivered his rifle to Howard and Miles. Twenty-six more Nez

Percé and twenty-seven soldiers had died at Bear Paws. In the Montana mountains the Oregon Nez Percé chief who did not want to go to Idaho uttered his immortal promise that "From where the sun now stands I will fight no more forever." [2]

Joseph agreed with Nelson Miles that the Nez Percé under him would return to the Lapwai Reservation, which is what Joseph had hoped for after the fight on the Clearwater. Miles had really not defeated the Nez Percé, for nearly one hundred warriors had escaped to Canada. Moreover, he failed to realize that Joseph was not his only opposing military commander. When Joseph gave up his rifle, he represented only himself and those who wished to follow him. According to Nez Percé traditions, other chiefs, such as Whitebird, could do as they pleased—and they did. Whitebird and many others crossed the international boundary into Canada.

Miles and Howard conceived of their pursuit of the Nez Percé as a war in military terms. According to their standards, a surrender would mean that the losing force would deliver up the troops and men to the victor as Lee did to Grant at Appomattox. However, American generals were forced to deal with the Nez Percé on Indian terms. The Nez Percé under Joseph did not surrender, they merely promised to do what they had reluctantly agreed to do at the first of the summer—go to the Lapwai Reservation. The Nez Percé under Whitebird, who went to Canada, were only completing the journey they had set out to achieve after leaving Yellowstone. Neither Joseph nor Whitebird was concerned about winning a war, only with trying to avoid one. That was their goal upon leaving Oregon, but it took nearly four months, a thousand miles, and hundreds of casualties to achieve that goal.

After traveling through some of the most difficult terrain in the Rocky Mountains to avoid battles and death, Joseph was now willing, as he had been in June, to go to the reservation. His oft-quoted speech to Miles signified that the sun was setting on an era of native American history. No more would the Nez

2. Merrill D. Beal, *"I Will Fight No More Forever": Chief Joseph and the Nez Percé War* (Seattle: University of Washington Press, 1963). Quotation taken from title of the book.

Percé freely travel from Oregon's Blue Mountains across Idaho's rugged Clearwater Mountains to Montana.

Unfortunately, the battlefield truce did not stand, and the Nez Percé were soon faced with the awful truth of their situation. Although Miles had agreed to send Joseph and the Nez Percé back to Idaho, he was superseded by higher authorities. The Nez Percé were taken to eastern Montana, to North Dakota, and Kansas before eventually arriving at a small reserve in Oklahoma. To mountain Indians, Oklahoma was an alien land among alien peoples.

After eight long years of attempting to cut his way through the governmental bureaucracy, Joseph, with the aid of his former adversary, Nelson Miles, finally managed to have the remnants of his people removed to either the Colville Reservation in eastern Washington or to Lapwai in Idaho. This was Joseph's great triumph, and as one historian has written, "that was a political, not a military victory." [3] The Nez Percé chief lived his remaining years at Colville and only visited at Lapwai.

Two more Indian confrontations ripped through Idaho before the end of the 1870s. Considering the proximity in both time and locale to the Nez Percé difficulties, it is somewhat amazing that none of the other Indian nations had helped the Nez Percé. They might have expected some aid from the Shoshonis, Lemhis, Bannocks, or Flatheads, but instead they found unfriendliness. In the case of the Lemhis and Bannocks, these tribes actually had provided scouts to assist the army in keeping up with the Nez Percé. An often-repeated device used by the army in fighting Indians was to capitalize on Indian animosities to gain allies against a certain tribe. The next year, the role of ally and enemy might be totally reversed, as illustrated by the case of the Bannocks in 1878. Buffalo Horn, a Bannock chief, had aided Howard in his pursuit of Joseph and the Nez Percé. A year later Buffalo Horn was leading an uprising, and Gen. O. O. Howard was in charge of the army operations against the Bannocks. No significant battles were fought; the casualties were certainly less;

3. Merle Wells, "The Nez Percé and Their War," *Pacific Northwest Quarterly* 55 (January 1964): 35–37.

but much of the southern part of Idaho was kept in a panic throughout that fall.

The Bannocks shared the Fort Hall Reservation with the Shoshoni and the conditions on the reservation led to a grasp for freedom on the part of the Bannocks. The reservation was poorly administered, and it seemed that whenever a competent, popular Indian agent was found, he soon would be replaced by one deemed incompetent. There was some animosity between the Bannock and Shoshoni because the Bannocks felt that the government officials favored the Shoshoni in the distribution of annuities. The Bannocks liked to wander from the reservation, and under the provisions of their treaty, they could go to the Camas Prairie annually. The fact that the government allowed white settlers to graze hogs, which rooted and destroyed the camas, on this traditional Indian gathering place, caused the Bannocks to think of leaving the reservation.

In the fall of 1877, individual Bannocks began shooting at freighters and settlers in and around Fort Hall. One man shot and wounded two freighters—perhaps because his sister had been raped by whites. The man was arrested, and while he was awaiting trial, another Bannock, Tambiago, shot and killed a white cattleman. More federal troops were sent to Fort Hall, and after a search of nearly two months, Tambiago was captured and sent to Malad for trial. Before he was executed, he told his captors that the decision of the Bannocks was for war. The officials at Fort Hall wanted to destroy the ability of the Bannocks to make trouble, so in midwinter the troops surrounded the Bannock villages and confiscated thirty-two rifles and nearly three hundred horses. Later, although local whites protested vigorously, the horses were returned, and most of the army units returned to Camp Douglas in Utah. As spring approached, the Bannocks prepared for their annual trek to Camas Prairie north of the Snake River in central Idaho. Much to the chagrin of the whites around Fort Hall, W. H. Danilson, the Indian agent, who did not have enough supplies to feed the Indians engaged in agriculture, did not feel that he could stop them and allowed them to leave. By early May, Buffalo Horn and the Bannocks had gathered on the Snake River.

Buffalo Horn had become a leader of the Bannock because of his scouting experience against other Indians. He had served under Generals George Crook and Nelson Miles during their 1876 operations against the Cheyennes. The next year, Buffalo Horn had joined Gen. O. O. Howard against the Nez Percé. Howard held the Bannock chief in high esteem—even though they did have their difficulties. Howard had been upset when Buffalo Horn and the other Bannocks disinterred the graves of Nez Percé at Big Hole in order to scalp them. At another time, the Bannock chief wanted to kill three Nez Percé herders who were accompanying Howard, but the army officer refused to permit it. Now this experienced ally of U. S. Army generals was to become their opponent.

All of the Bannocks joined Chief Tendoy's Lemhis at Camas Prairie, and instead of the roots they sought they found the hogs, cattle, and horses of whites. Upset by the destruction to the Camas root, Buffalo Horn told the herders to take their animals and leave immediately. The whites did as advised and probably saved their lives. On May 28, two young Bannocks, after a drinking and gambling spree, went into the cattlemen's camp and, with no provocation, shot and wounded two men. The territory was soon alarmed at the prospect of another Indian war.

After a council of war, Buffalo Horn knew that all of the people were not for war. He allowed some of the Bannocks to return to Fort Hall immediately, and the Lemhis left to avoid even the appearance of collusion with the Bannocks. Buffalo Horn, who realized that the wrath of the government would be exercised on all Bannocks, convinced the remaining Bannocks to go with him on the warpath for as long as possible. Approximately one hundred and fifty experienced warriors joined him now in an attempt to steal supplies and horses and regain what the whites had taken.

In search of allies, about forty Bannocks crossed into Oregon and, at the northern Paiute Malheur Reservation, asked for rations from the agent. When he refused, the Paiute chief, Egan, gave the Bannocks some food, and then they left together. A few days later, some of the farming Indians left Malheur and joined Egan and the visiting Bannocks. The northern Paiutes had grievances similar to those of the Bannock. Their main problem was the Indian agent, W. V. Rinehart, who lacked integrity and seemed both inefficient and corrupt. When Egan did not return for the next week's rations, an apprehensive Rinehart abandoned the agency and moved into a settlement.

Meanwhile, Buffalo Horn had been ravaging the countryside along the Snake River. The Bannocks had raided King Hill Station on the old Oregon Trail, and at Glenn's Ferry, they raided another station and then crossed into Bruneau valley and the rugged country of southwestern Idaho. They left behind at least five dead whites and took with them hundreds of horses. Under Howard's direction, troops left Fort Boise and attempted to pick up the trail of the Bannocks. The regular army was joined by several Idaho militia detachments hastily organized by Idaho's leaders. Faced with unfavorable numerical odds, the Bannocks attempted to avoid their pursuers as they continued toward Oregon and a rendezvous with Egan's Paiutes.

On June 8, about sixty Bannocks engaged in a skirmish with militiamen from Silver City, and several Indians were killed. Buffalo Horn, the experienced war chieftain, was wounded. Four days later, the chief was dead. A Paiute scout, working for the whites, claimed credit for killing the Bannock chief. The remainder of the Bannocks joined the Paiutes and held a council. The Bannocks wanted a total war, but many Paiutes, especially Winnemucca, were for peace. Finally Egan, convinced that the only way to get better treatment and more rations was to go on the warpath, assumed the leadership of the combined Bannock-Paiute forces.

General Howard was now in personal command of the army, and he directed several units in pursuit of the Indians. The army never could achieve a situation where a complete battle could be conducted. Only a series of skirmishes resulted as the Bannocks-Paiutes tried to get the Umatillas and Cayuses to join them. The Umatillas remained on the agency, and some of them, tempted by a rumored reward for the capture of Egan, feigned a union with Egan in order to capture him. Once surrounded, Egan attempted escape, but was shot and then scalped.

THE SNAKE THROUGH IDAHO

A photographer's essay by Bob Peterson

Leaderless, the Bannocks engaged in elusive measures to return to Idaho and avoid capture.

The remaining small bands crossed through the Salmon River Mountains and killed a few prospectors who happened to be in their path. In order to avoid capture and punishment, some of the Bannocks joined the Lemhis, and a few slipped back into Fort Hall. Others, now dreaming of joining Sitting Bull, pressed into Wyoming and Montana, where one group was annihilated by troops under Nelson A. Miles. By October, the Bannock War was over, and the Indian combatants were either dead, locked up in army cells from Montana to Nebraska, or back at Fort Hall. In a last great frustrated show of bitterness, the Bannocks had chosen to follow Buffalo Horn in an act of resentment against those who had despoiled their country. Their failure and tragedy was compounded the next year when the final major Indian-white confrontation occurred. Ironically, it started over the deaths of another persecuted Idaho minority, the Chinese.

High in the rugged mountains of central Idaho lived an unknown number of Indians who were called Sheepeaters by the other Indians. Traditionally horseless, they roamed through the mountains of the Salmon River drainage living off the varieties of big game. The area they inhabited included what is now the spectacular Idaho Primitive Area and the Sawtooth Wilderness and Recreation areas. Equipped with excellent hunting equipment and well-trained dogs, they ate well throughout the year. They were also fantastic furriers who tanned hides with careful precision. The result was splendidly beautiful fur clothes. The mountain sheep, fox, badger, coyote, antelope, wolf, and elk were all utilized. Living by themselves in difficult terrain, they had a limited domain, sharing almost none of it with whites.

As early as 1866, miners had moved into Sheepeater territory and caused damage to the fish and game resources. Because the Indians retaliated by stealing horses or other belongings from the miners, the Sheepeaters were classed as renegades and outlaws. In reality, they were a disorganized nomadic people who were desirous of protecting their homeland. Another interesting point is that in the violence-prone, well-armed mining camps, most atrocities were blamed on Indians if there happened to be any in the vicinity—which was probably the case in the incident that sent federal troops on a campaign that ended when the Sheepeaters moved onto the Fort Hall Reservation.

During February 1879, five Chinese miners were killed and robbed on Loon Creek, about one hundred miles northeast of Boise. Upon hearing of this incident, General Howard ordered federal troops stationed at Boise and Grangeville to converge on the Salmon River Mountains and find out who the murderers were. It was assumed that the perpetrators of the crime were Indians; otherwise the local white authorities would have investigated. Soon more than one hundred armed troopers, in three different detachments, were battling the late spring snows in an attempt to find the Sheepeaters. The small band of mountain Indians probably numbered less than one hundred.

After the experiences of the Nez Percé and the Bannocks, the Sheepeaters decided to resist the armed invasion of the Salmon River drainage. As one part of the cavalry under Lt. Henry Catley proceeded up Big Creek east of McCall, they were ambushed by approximately a dozen Sheepeaters. As the army attempted retreat, one Sheepeater warrior pinned them down. After other braves joined him, they kept over sixty soldiers, scouts, and packers under siege for fourteen hours. Only after discarding their baggage were the troops able to escape from the battle of "Vinegar Hill." After seven weeks in the field, Catley returned empty handed and was ordered to join the forces under Capt. Reuben Bernard at the mouth of Elk Creek on the Salmon's South Fork.

In the meantime, small groups of Sheepeaters had attacked ranches in the vicinity of Warrens near the south fork. A few ranchers had been killed and these depredations added justification for the increased use of the military. Still, it was no easy task to corner the Sheepeaters in the mountains they knew so well.

In mid-August, Bernard and his large force of cavalry finally caught up with the Sheepeaters farther down Big Creek, near the Middle Fork of the Salmon. After a brief skirmish, the Indians fled down the middle fork, but had to abandon most of their belongings. Bernard was in a position where he could have forced a Sheepeater truce, but he decided not to pursue. He concluded that the cavalry horses could not make it through the canyons. Already many horses and mules had collapsed from sheer exhaustion and had been shot. Bernard ordered a retreat, and most of the cavalry returned to Boise.

Bernard, estimating the total number of Sheepeater warriors at thirty, allowed two lieutenants, E. S. Farrow and W. S. Brown, to remain in the field with twenty-three soldiers and approximately twenty Umatilla scouts. For nearly a month, they pursued the elusive Indians through the increasingly difficult terrain. Without the time to hunt or fish, the Sheepeaters became more destitute and demoralized. After crossing numerous ranges and hundreds of miles, a single Sheepeater, Tamanmo, came to Farrow and Brown and discussed the terms of peace. Although Tamanmo claimed that the Sheepeaters had not participated in the murders on Loon Creek, he agreed to end the flight and go with the troops to a reservation. Within a few days, he was back with approximately fifty other Indians, mostly women and children. Some of the Sheepeaters remained in the mountains and one chief, Eagle Eye, did not move to Fort Hall for many years.

Thus the campaign ended without a significant or defined battle. Although the expeditions and searches lasted for nearly a half year, at the most the Sheepeaters did not have more than twenty-five warriors. The Sheepeaters who abandoned the mountains and returned with the troops were taken to Grangeville, then to Lapwai, and to the Umatilla agency in Oregon. After wintering at Vancouver Barracks, they were returned to Idaho in the spring of 1880 and settled with the Shoshonis and Bannocks at Fort Hall. The troops returned to their various commands, and Idaho's Indian wars had ended. There were then six reservations and nowhere did the Indian freedom of an earlier day exist.

The Indian attempt to change their status by revolting was inevitable, and for nearly twenty years, Idaho Territory was the scene of numerous massacres, battles, skirmishes, and tragedies. The final solution was a white solution based on immediate desires and ambitions of the predominant white culture. Reservations meant that previously inaccessible lands could now be opened for mining, grazing, or tilling. For the Indians, confined to acreage unfamiliar and restrictive, the options were now closed. Their way of life was to undergo a profound cultural shock that led to a continued miserable and distasteful existence on a small reservation. For people who freely roamed, this was a poor solution—one that still cries for impossible answers.

By 1880, Idaho's remaining native Americans were tucked away on the six different reservations, totaling well over two million acres. Ninety years later, Indian population had increased slightly, but the reservation acreage had decreased to around eight hundred thousand acres, and the Lemhi Reservation had been terminated. These five remaining reservations are a haunting reminder of man's atrocities against man played out in an Idaho, as well as a national, setting.

Fort Hall was constructed by the trader, Nathaniel Wyeth, at the spot where the Oregon Trail meets the Snake River in southeastern Idaho. It was a significant and needed provisioning point for Oregon-bound travelers. Now the trading post has left its name to Idaho's most populous Indian reservation. Presently, approximately three thousand Shoshonis and Bannocks live there. Other major Shoshoni reservations are in western Nevada and central Wyoming. Mostly sagebrush-covered foothills and gentle mountains, the Fort Hall reservation and the area surrounding it was the traditional home for the Bannocks and some Shoshonis. These mountain lands produce enormous quantities of phosphate ore, and modern irrigation techniques create well-watered circles of green crops on the flat, once desert acres. But mineral and agricultural leases are often controlled by gigantic agribusiness concerns. Little of the phosphate mining or agricultural prosperity is felt by the Shoshonis. According to census bureau statistics, the suicide rate at Fort Hall is exceptionally high, and the general feeling of the inhabitants has been one of frustration and despair. The original acreage set aside in 1867 was 1.8 million, but that has dwindled to approximately one-half million. Concerted efforts are being made through the courts to return to the Shoshoni-Bannock land they claim was taken from them illegally.

Nearly three hundred miles southwest of Fort Hall is a small reservation located on the Idaho-Nevada border at Duck Valley. A handful of northern Paiutes, sometimes called Snakes and Bannocks, are located in this isolated mountain valley. Originally, these Paiutes roamed from eastern Oregon and western Idaho through northern Nevada to the Sierra Nevada. Approximately two hundred of these Indians live on the Idaho side of the reservation. Descendants of what whites derisively referred to as Digger Indians, their existence is meager, and their mountain lands supply the bare necessities of survival.

Although the Nez Percé Indians used to move freely from the Bitterroot Mountains on the east to Oregon's Blue Mountains in the west, they are presently confined on a reservation east of Lewiston on the Clearwater River. This is the area that Joseph's Nez Percé had tried to avoid, but where many of them finally settled. Numerous towns are contained in this well-watered and fertile agricultural area. The site of the Henry Spalding mission to the Nez Percé is within the current confines of the reservation, but the Clearwater battleground of the Nez Percé War is a few miles east of the border. In excess of two thousand Nez Percé remain near Lapwai, the center of the agency's activities.

Two smaller reservations are located in the Panhandle of northern Idaho. The Coeur d'Alene Indians have a beautiful location south and west of Coeur d'Alene Lake for their reservation and nearly eight hundred native Americans reside there. With difficulty the Coeur d'Alenes have been able to maintain an identity in many of the smaller Panhandle towns. Farther north, near the Canadian boundary, is the Kootenai Reservation. There are only about eighty Kootenais living along the banks of the Kootenai River as it winds its way northward. Most of this tribe live in adjacent areas of Montana or Canada.

These five reservations and adjacent communities are where most of Idaho's seven thousand contemporary Indians reside. Rarely, if ever, has the population of the native Americans in Idaho exceeded that number. Currently, the Indian population comprises less than one-hundredth of the total population; yet the Indian imprint on Idaho is permanent and positive. Eventually, the new materialistic exploitive white culture they confronted overwhelmed them.

Now nearly one hundred years later, it is becoming obvious

that much good could have been gleaned from the native American culture. Their traditional respect and reverence for nature is needed now in a dramatic way. The pace of life and the appreciation of its cycles could save many citizens on the path toward cardiac arrest. But these are wishful thoughts, mere blowing in the wind. Industrial mining and the civilizing effect of statehood were on Idaho's horizon as Joseph gave in, the Bannocks were caught, and the Sheepeaters made their way into Fort Hall.

5

The Creation of a State:
Railroads and Mines

*F*OR twenty-seven years, 1863–1890, Idaho was a territorial ward of the federal government. The census of 1890 claimed there was no longer a defined frontier line, and Idaho's admission to statehood that year is symbolic of the passing frontier. These were the national years of great industrial growth when massive fortunes were obtained by an unbridled exploitation of the natural resources. While the Rockefellers, Harrimans, Hills, Goulds, Carnegies, and Vanderbilts were accumulating unbelievable amounts of wealth, Idaho was becoming not only a part of the nation, but was contributing to these vast industrial complexes.

By 1890, when Idaho became the forty-third state, the population had increased to 88,548, political parties and institutions had been established, and most parts of the state were connected by a network of freighting roads and eastern-financed railroads. These were also the years of great lead-silver strikes of the Wood River and the Coeur d'Alenes, which brought industrial corporate mining to the mountains of central and northern Idaho. The territorial period is significant because it highlights the human and ecological problems that concern Idahoans in 1976. Three main themes evolve out of Idaho's territorial history. One highlights the political problems of being governed by

91

Washington, D.C., and of a growing virulent anti-Mormonism. The second theme concerns the development of transportation and communication linkages backed by eastern capital. The final theme dramatizes mineral exploitation and labor's reaction to it. These divergent forces brought statehood to Idaho and charted the course for the twentieth century.

Anytime a distant territory is governed by political appointees of a patronage-oriented president, there is the potential for trouble. This is especially true when the appointees have never seen the territory they are asked to govern. Idaho territory was not a lush prize sought by many spoilsmen. Republicans held the White House for all but four years of Idaho's territorial history and no matter who made the appointment—Lincoln, Johnson, Grant, Hayes, or Arthur—it was never popular in Idaho. Sixteen different men were appointed to the governorship, twelve actually served, but six of the twelve spent less than a year in the area. The last two governors appointed, E. A. Stevenson and George Shoup, were pioneer residents of Idaho and that fact deflected much early resentment. However, all of Idaho's territorial problems—religious, political, or military— were often blamed on these alien carpetbag governors. Accused by Idahoans of corruption, fraud, theft, speculation, and conflict of interest, the governors rarely remained in office for their full four-year terms. At times the allegations were true, to a degree, because some federal appointees were guilty of fraud and corruption. Caleb Lyon was accused of embezzling more than forty thousand dollars and Thomas Bennett of election fraud.

In reality, federal officials in Idaho were plagued by two nagging problems. On the one hand, the salaries paid were so low that most governors had to hold another job or speculate to survive. From 1877–1890, the annual salary was $2,600. On the other hand, Idaho was a Democratic territory politically. Republican-appointed federal officials were watched by, and forced to contend with, Democratic legislatures throughout the territorial period. The main protest against the governors, judges, marshals, and land office agents was political. At times, the protest was merely a cover to hide the deep internal political wars, sectional rivalries, and anti-Mormon bigotry. Perhaps the greatest reason for local distaste for federal officers was the desire for statehood and home rule. Men appointed by the president of the United States were the demons to be fought by those in the young, politically immature territory. Who controlled the patronage was the key to many politicians' happiness, and until locals were appointed throughout the territory, the concept of carpetbagging was decried. However local issues, such as the Mormon controversy, made Idaho's territorial political history unique.

During the territorial period, the Mormons continued to plant communities throughout southern Idaho. When Brigham Young died in 1877, there were over thirty distinct Mormon settlements in Idaho. With the completion of the Utah and Northern Railroad north into the upper Snake River valley, the tie between Salt Lake City and these Idaho colonies became a fact. There were a number of things that made the Mormons particularly obnoxious to other state residents, but foremost was the church's belief in male plural marriage, usually referred to as polygamy instead of polygyny. Because of this doctrine, many residents of Idaho had more than one wife and numerous offspring. Even most Mormons who did not adopt the practice stoutly defended their comrades who were involved. As a vital part of the Church of Jesus Christ of Latter-day Saint theology, Mormons believed that plural marriage, if followed righteously, could lead to individual and family exaltation. However, to the nonbeliever, polygamy was a despicable doctrine that satisfied the sinful desires of dirty old men masquerading as church leaders.

Added to the volatile issue of plural marriage was the traditional voting pattern of the Mormons. From their earliest history in Ohio, Missouri, and Illinois, the saints had usually voted as a bloc. In Idaho, they held the balance of power from 1872 until 1882, when an anti-Mormon combine began to win elections. Usually the Idaho Mormons voted Democratic, so for most of the territorial period, they supported the winner. As long as Mormons voted, they remained Democrats, and in Cassia, Bear Lake, and Oneida counties, they could usually elect territorial representatives of their own faith. Consequently, with the political issue of voting tied to the moral issue of marriage, Idaho became the scene of some strange events. However, the climax of the struggle between the Mormons and the rest of Idaho was reached in part because of national legislation.

In 1862, Congress passed the Morrill Anti-bigamy Act at the same time it was approving the Homestead Act and the financing of a transcontinental railroad. The law, however, which provided for fine and imprisonment of a man if convicted of bigamy, was ineffective because a wife could not testify against her husband and witnesses were sworn to secrecy. Still, the federal government continued to pursue a course designed to rid the nation of one of the "relics of barbarism." Another law was passed that allowed for non-Mormon juries to be brought in on polygamy trials.

Between 1880 and 1882 rumors were circulated throughout southern Idaho that elected Mormons took their orders from Salt Lake City and had little regard at all for Idaho. The Independent party of Oneida County was formed to oppose church-supported candidates and legislation. In late 1880, territorial Gov. John B. Neil proposed that an Idaho law be passed that would permit officers to arrest persons who even advocated plural marriage. Any evidence of cohabitation could be used as proof of polygamy.

With the prevailing mood in Idaho becoming strikingly anti-Mormon, the scene was set for politicians to move toward complete Mormon disfranchisement. One man was in the wings and waiting for his chance at center stage. Fred T. Dubois was the moving force behind the eventual victory of the anti-Mormon forces.

After attending Yale, Dubois had come to Idaho with his brother and for two years had worked at Fort Hall until he became United States marshal. Congress delivered to Dubois the necessary tools for victory over the Mormons when it passed the Edmunds Act in 1882. The Edmunds Act said that a person could be convicted of illegal cohabitation, which made it unnecessary to prove the existence of a formal polygamous marriage. The legislation also disqualified any practitioner of polygamy from voting, holding office, or serving as a juror in cases involving plural marriage. Dubois now used a variety of techniques to convict Mormons and disfranchise them. All Dubois needed was to prove that a man visited a woman with the same last name, that she charged goods to his account, and that she could not prove the parentage of her children. The all-anti-Mormon juries, which were permitted, would convict on the above-named evidence.

The crafty marshal had greater personal goals than to convict polygamists. Dubois wanted to relegate the Idaho Democratic party to a minority position by associating it with the Mormons and simultaneously elevating himself to a position of prominence among territorial Republicans. In other words, Dubois and his followers used the polygamy issue to gain recruits for their political party, the Anti-Mormon party of Oneida County, which ultimately merged with the Republicans. Dubois also was interested in curbing the political influence of the Utah-based church in Idaho politics. The fact that the church attempted to dictate voting preferences added fuel to Dubois's charges.

In the Idaho election of 1884, Dubois's party used fraud, intimidation, deceit, chicanery, and the courts to win in Oneida County and unseat the Mormons. Dubois's chief supporter, A. W. Smith, was elected to the legislature and became chairman of the Judiciary Committee. Smith hurriedly drafted a bill that was designed to deny the vote to all Mormons, not just those involved in plural marriage. The anti-Mormon legislation went beyond the Edmunds Act by stipulating that anyone who practiced, believed, taught, advocated, or supported polygamy would be disfranchised. Smith's bill also provided for the disfranchisement of any person who belonged to an organization that believed in plural marriage. As part of the enforcement provision, the Idaho Test Oath was attached, which meant that anyone challenged had to testify under oath that he did not belong to the Mormon church or believe in its doctrines. The Test Oath Act was passed and became law in early 1885. Politically, the Mormons were no longer a force in Idaho. Naturally, they fought the act in the courts, but while they resorted to legal procedures, the church members were in effect voteless. All Mormons, unless they denounced their religion, would be removed from the Idaho legislature, even those representatives from communities that were almost completely Mormon.

The territorial and national courts upheld Dubois in his crusade to destroy the Democrats and politically muzzle the Mormons. In 1885, the U. S. Supreme Court in *Clawson* v. *The United States* ruled that the exclusion of Mormons from juries deciding cases of polygamy and unlawful cohabitation was proper and legal. Dubois's practice of selecting jurors with no specified requirement, other than anti-Mormonism, was upheld. These court cases gave Dubois the green light to push into southern Idaho and use every available means to catch Mormon polygamists. Finally, in a series of cases between 1888 and 1890, the Idaho and the national supreme courts decided on the constitutionality of the Idaho Test Oath Act. In each instance, the test oath was ruled constitutional and the courts upheld the right of a state to determine its internal voting qualifications. Consequently, the Test Oath Act was not ruled an infringement of religious freedom nor a violation of individual civil rights.

Encouraged by the court decision in the Clawson case, Dubois decided to ride the wave of anti-Mormonism into the halls of Congress. As a Republican, he was elected by a narrow margin over John Hailey in a verbally violent campaign. Maintaining his commitment to oppose Mormons as citizens, Dubois, as the congressional delegate, cleverly worked toward Idaho's statehood.

Idaho's two resident territorial governors, E. A. Stevenson, a Democrat, and his successor, George L. Shoup, a Republican, called and brought together a bipartisan constitutional convention in 1890. Stevenson initiated the movement and Shoup carried it through to the final document. Expediency was the order of the day and the election of delegates was most unusual. In one case, three men elected themselves to the convention. Naturally, the Mormons were excluded completely, and the Test Oath Act became part of the new state's constitution. In fact, the Republicans insisted on repelling any future attempts by the Mormons to vote by giving the state legislature the power to disfranchise anyone. The convention tried to placate northern Idaho, which had been involved in a Washington annexation movement, by declaring that the state's university should be in Moscow. In November, Idaho's voters overwhelmingly supported the constitution, anti-Mormon provisions and all. The document was then forwarded to Congress with the formal statehood request.

Idaho's petition for statehood was granted speedily. With the slightest of majorities, a Republican Congress was desirous of admitting new states that would elect Republican representatives. Thomas Reed ("the Czar") was Speaker of the House, and by utilizing underhanded methods that included declaring a quorum present, even though the Democrats refused to answer the roll call, the Idaho admission act was passed on to the Senate. With limited debate, the Senate approved the act, and President Benjamin Harrison signed it on July 3, 1890. The forty-third star was now ready to be etched onto the national flag, even if a large number of Idaho citizens were disfranchised because of their religion.

Even though the Mormon church was pressured into abandoning polygamy in September of 1890, the first Idaho state legislature still prevented the LDS people from voting. Dubois, who became one of Idaho's United States senators, switched from the Republicans to the Democrats over the free silver issue and the candidacy of William Jennings Bryan in 1896. He took his dedicated anti-Mormonism philosophy with him, and was still Mormon-baiting in the first decade of the twentieth century. By 1896, the Idaho legislature restored the vote to the Mormons, who were able to vote against their old nemesis, Dubois, in 1896, 1900, and 1906. Ironically, by the mid-1890s, some Mormon leaders had become political bedfellows of Dubois.

Obviously, the Mormon issue and politics were not the only problems faced by Idaho as it progressed through territorial status. Still sparsely populated and isolated from the east and west by mountains and rugged terrain, a transportation and communication transformation occurred which brought all of Idaho closer together. By the first decade of the twentieth century, four major railroad lines crossed Idaho connecting it to the West Coast and the Midwest. In addition, a major line stretched from Utah through eastern Idaho to the Montana mines. Branch lines were spreading from the main lines into numerous mining towns and villages. These railroads had an enormous economic impact on the state by opening the area to settlers and in carrying agricultural and mineral products to a wider market.

Prior to the advent of the railroad, placer miners usually followed the well-worn Indian trails. However, when lode mining developed, it was necessary to have a better mode of transportation. Steamboats operating on the Columbia River and on California's Sacramento River supplied Idaho to a limited degree during the early territorial years. Freighters and stagecoach companies connected the river terminals to the Idaho towns. Numerous ferries were operated across the rivers, and stage stations sprang up along the overland trail. The completion of the transcontinental railroad affected Idaho to a great degree. Although the original line passed south of Idaho's borders, it provided closer rail access for Idaho's freighters. Many railroad towns in northern Nevada and Utah became the centers of supply for Idaho. It would only be a matter of time before rails supplanted the rutted wagon roads into Idaho.

The Utah Northern Railroad first crossed into Idaho at Franklin in May of 1874. Built by Cache valley Mormons, with some eastern capital, this narrow-gauge line was designed to connect the northern Mormon settlements to the original transcontinental line near Brigham City. The financiers hoped that the line would eventually reach the Montana mines. By 1876 the line had extended northward to the site of the Battle of Bear River. External economic factors, caused by the national panic of 1873, caused the Utah Northern promoters to sell the small line with its equipment to the noted railroad mogul, Jay Gould. Gould persuaded his Union Pacific partners that when the line reached the Montana mines, it would turn a fabulous profit—so the new Utah and Northern came into being. The Gould interests paid only $100,000 for the property at foreclosure rates. Construction was resumed, and by 1882 the tracks had arrived at the terminus in Garrison, Montana. The line was 466 miles long with nearly half of the trackage in Idaho. The surveyed and completed line ran through the heart of the Fort Hall Reservation. Railroad officials were able to negotiate an agreement with the government that allowed them almost free access to Indian lands, and, as compensation, the reservation Indians were offered free rides within the reservation.

By 1882, the Utah and Northern was returning earnings in excess of two million dollars, but, more importantly, it hastened the settlement of eastern Idaho. That same year many Mormons were asked by the church to leave Utah, take their belongings, and move to the upper Snake River valley. At the very time the anti-Mormon crusade was beginning to bear political fruit for Fred Dubois, thousands of Mormons were plowing the land and establishing communities from Blackfoot to Victor in famous Pierre's Hole. Because of the railroad, these colonization efforts were relatively easy. Wild rumors were circulated about proposed extensions of the Utah and Northern across the territory to Boise, but that task was left for another division of the Union Pacific.

Eighteen eighty-two was also the year the Oregon Short Line came to Idaho. Union Pacific officials decided to connect their transcontinental line to the Northwest, and proposed a line from Granger, Wyoming, across Idaho to Oregon, where it would connect with the Oregon Railway and Navigation Company. The suggested route would roughly correspond with the legendary Oregon Trail. For the most part this was familiar terrain that would not provide unusual natural obstacles. There was no need to follow the Snake River when the construction proved difficult. (For most of the way, the railbed was built on the north side of the river; whereas the main wagon route had been on the south side all the way to Glenn's Ferry.) When completed, it would mean that all of southern Idaho would be served by a transcontinental railroad. Because of the infamous Crédit Mobilier scandal, the Union Pacific people could not count on the federal government to assist with the financing either by land grant or by mileage compensation. Instead, the Union Pacific leadership under Charles Francis Adams, Jr., offered Oregon Short Line Stock to UP shareholders and organized the Idaho and Oregon Land Improvement Company. This company, which included Andrew Mellon as one of the directors, and United States Senator Alexander Caldwell of Kansas as president, was given advance notice of places where stations would be located. The land company surveyed the townsites and promoted the sale of the surrounding acreage. Half of the profits were returned to the railroad. Large amounts of federal land were obtained by the land company, on which they attracted some colonization, but without a guaranteed water supply, farmers were reluctant to settle the area. Initially, the arrangement between the two companies worked well, but after some limited development the agreement was terminated. (One reason for the cessation of co-operation was that the railroad did well on its own. The Oregon Short Line made quick profits once they built a branch line from Shoshone to Hailey and the Wood River mines.) The tracks were laid quickly, and by February 1884, the line was completed into Oregon. It spanned the mighty Snake four times and originally bypassed the territorial capital in Boise because of the grade drop into the city. Counting the spur to Hailey, over five hundred miles of track had been constructed in Idaho by the Oregon Short Line.

The completion of the railroad through Idaho to Oregon brought about a communication revolution. In 1884 it was possible to board the train in Omaha, Nebraska, on Monday and arrive in Portland, Oregon, the following Friday. It had taken Lewis and Clark over eighteen months to make a similar trip eighty years previously, and Oregon Trail pioneers had hoped to make it in four months only forty years earlier. Shortly after the completion, the E. H. Harriman family traveled to Shoshone and explored the surrounding area, thus sowing the seeds for the development of Sun Valley in the 1930s. Jay Gould also spent many summers in the Idaho mountains serviced by his Union Pacific combine.

Numerous other small feeder lines were constructed throughout southern Idaho. When the Utah and Northern temporarily merged with the Oregon Short Line from McCammon to Pocatello, Pocatello became the "Gate City" to the West Coast or Montana. As a railroad community, Pocatello became a center for non-Mormons in heavily Mormon southeastern Idaho. The town grew rapidly and provided some unique cultural alternatives. Some black Americans moved into Pocatello and worked for the railroad. Many of the twenty-five hundred blacks currently in Idaho trace their origins to the railroad and the minor industrialization that accompanied its arrival. The railroads and the types of people who worked on them caused great concern among heavily Mormon communities. In Montpelier, the tensions between the Mormons and the railroaders grew to such proportions that a fence was actually constructed between the two sections of town, and separate schools were maintained. These cultural and social reactions to the railroad were not felt in other areas, especially in the thin Panhandle where three transcontinental lines eventually crossed on their way to the Pacific Coast. Idaho was not the destination of any major line, but once again presented natural obstacles that slowed down the advancing transportation frontier.

The Northern Pacific was completed with considerable fanfare in the autumn of 1883. Henry Villard, an eccentric and energetic Oregonian, assumed the leadership of this road which was to connect Portland to Saint Paul. Although its transit across Idaho was of limited mileage, the route was through some extremely rough terrain. Indeed, the engineers had a difficult time in deciding how to build the line through Idaho Territory. Finally, they concluded that the only way was to go through mountains rather than around them. The completed tracks crossed Idaho along Pend Oreille Lake and across the Rathdrum Prairie over a route that had no large mountains to climb. A one-mile tunnel was gouged out, and by the spring of 1882 the Idaho section was completed. When the rails were joined in Montana, Villard added an international flavor to the festivities by inviting royalty and diplomats from Europe as well as German scholars to attend. Former President Ulysses S. Grant gave a speech and struck a spike, but the event was fourteen years too late to capture the public imagination. The Northern Pacific built branch lines down into the southern Panhandle of Idaho and eventually up the Clearwater River. These lines helped precipitate the growth of the lumber industry.

Ten years later, a salty and rugged Canadian, James J. Hill, achieved his transcontinental desire by completing the Great Northern Railroad, which tied Duluth, Minnesota, on Lake Superior to Everett, Washington, on the Puget Sound. This line crossed the Idaho Panhandle by following the Kootenai River from Montana through a rugged corkscrew canyon and then veering south and west into Washington. The Great Northern construction crew was delayed significantly by the Kootenai River Canyon. They finally were forced to blast a right-of-way out of the rock on the southern wall. While this was a majestic engineering feat, it certainly damaged the beauty of a wild river and its centuries-old canyon. Hill built an empire along his designated route as his workers laid the track. Scandinavian immigrants were sold the land as the railroad moved across the Dakotas and Montana. Hill constructed feeder lines all along the way, and an entire economic network was the final result. Hill's methods proved so successful that when the severe economic panic of 1893 hit, and he was just completing the Great Northern, his company paid a 5 percent dividend and had a surplus of over a million dollars. The rival Northern Pacific was in such dire straits that Hill simply absorbed that line into his already successful system.

A third northern railroad, the Chicago, Milwaukee, Saint Paul, and Pacific, was also competed in the Northwest, but had a shaky financial history. Completed by 1910, this road probably found the easiest route into northern Idaho. After leaving Missoula, Montana, it followed the Clark Fork River until the river turned eastward. The railroad entered Idaho near Mullan, and then pursued a course to the Saint Maries River and on to Spokane. Designed to compete with the Hill-Harriman forces of the Great Northern and Union Pacific, the Chicago, Milwaukee, Saint Paul, and Pacific never displaced them nor did it succeed as well economically.

Perhaps the major significance of the railroads in northern Idaho was their contribution to the development of lead-silver lode mining in the area of the Coeur d'Alenes. The whole idea of industrial lode mining in Idaho was changed by the railroads. The necessary heavy equipment could be shipped directly to the mining sites, and the ore could be carried to smelters in Omaha or Salt Lake City and then to the marketplace. Just as the railroads had to be financed by outside capital, the same was true of the great silver-lead mines of Wood River and the Coeur d'Alenes.

Indian difficulties had kept many miners out of the rugged mountains of central Idaho for nearly two decades, but once the Bannocks and Sheepeaters were safely on the Fort Hall Reservation, the rush into the majestic Boulder, Soldier, and Sawtooth mountains began. As early as 1864, Warren Callahan had found a galena lode on the upper Wood River—but Callahan was interested in gold, not lead sulphide. Fifteen years later, Callahan had changed his mind. Profitable techniques for smelting silver and lead ores had been developed in Nevada and Colorado, and the transportation revolution of the railroad was underway. Joined by numerous other prospecters, Callahan returned to the Wood River in 1879, and soon lead-silver mines dotted the surrounding mountains. After sending out ore samples for testing, Callahan, David Ketchum, Frank Jacobs, and about forty miners wintered in the mountains.

Thousands of hungry fortune seekers hit the Wood River valley the next spring. Communities such as Ketchum, Bellevue, and Hailey all boomed with the success of the numerous mines. John Hailey, who owned the Utah, Idaho, and Oregon Stage Company, which served the mines until the rails arrived, became a prominent land and mine promoter. As an official of the Idaho and Oregon Land Improvement Company, a Union Pacific subsidiary, Hailey could use vast capital resources to promote the trading center that bore his name. Among his backers was Andrew Mellon, a company officer and later secretary of the treasury during the 1920s. This same company planned and developed other Idaho communities, including Mountain Home and Caldwell.

Once the Oregon Short Line hit Hailey in 1883, the boom was on. Literally millions of dollars worth of ore were taken from the hills, and the ore was either smelted at small plants in the valley or shipped to established smelters. A Philadelphia-based firm established a large smelter in Ketchum which proved to be successful. With added eastern capital, including some Jay Gould money, the mines were developed and worked extensively. E. A. Wall purchased the Bullion Mine in 1882 for

$200,000. Pouring development capital into the mine and using the latest techniques of mining, late in 1882 Wall shipped out $668,000 worth of ore in forty days. Wall's was not an atypical investment. The largest of the early producers was a mine called the Minnie Moore, located near Bellevue. A director of the Bank of England bought the Minnie Moore for nearly a half million dollars in 1884. The mine eventually returned millions for the investors. British capital was also used to buy the Bullion Mine for over a million dollars, and the foreigners did not lose on this purchase. By the end of the 1880s, while Fred Dubois and others were working for statehood, approximately twenty million dollars worth of silver and lead had been extracted from the Wood River mines. Another mine, the Triumph, was discovered southeast of Ketchum in 1884, and, although it took over forty years to achieve major production, its wealth ultimately surpassed the rest of the Wood River mines combined.

All of these developments took place when the United States was beginning to undergo a whole series of communication and transportation revolutions. During the peak years of the Wood River rush, Hailey operated three daily newspapers, and Bellevue, five miles away, had two. Hailey was the first Idaho community to utilize the telephone, and along with Ketchum pioneered the use of electric lights. The effect of the iron rails that tied the nation together and sped communications was felt in Idaho by the 1880s. By the end of the decade, when statehood was granted, Idaho was in reality an important part of the nation. Especially was this true after the highly publicized lead-silver-zinc strikes in the Coeur d'Alenes, and the subsequent labor problems, gained national attention.

The year 1882 is one of the most significant years in Idaho history. Fred Dubois was disfranchising Mormons, the Oregon Short Line entered Idaho, the Northern Pacific was completed across Idaho, the Wood River mines were producing spectacularly, and A. J. Pritchard, a so-called freethinker from Montana, located a quartz claim a few miles from present-day Kellogg, Idaho. The lead-silver district that resulted from Pritchard's find is the largest in the United States. More than two billion dollars worth of lead, silver, and zinc has been taken from the hills of the Coeur d'Alenes. In the process, the Coeur d'Alenes have been stripped and tunneled, resulting in barren hillsides, mammoth tailings, and polluting smelters. In the age-old battle between exploitation and preservation or restoration, Idaho's Coeur d'Alene lead and silver mines illustrate the need for balance.

As a consequence of Pritchard's discovery, significant national labor and mining history was made. Pritchard intended to keep his claim secret until many of his fellow Liberal League members (freethinkers) could join him and file adjacent twenty-acre claims. Pritchard was able to keep knowledge of the find from the general public until the fall of 1883. But by the following winter, the opportunistic Northern Pacific was flooding the nation with circulars advertising the strike east of Coeur d'Alene Lake. As prospectors found ore, numerous boom towns lined the canyons, and Murray, Mullan, Burke, and Osburn became mining entities. However, the biggest strikes were still to come.

Noah Kellogg, who had been a builder in Murray, left that village in 1885 and decided to prospect for gold. Unemployed and sixty years of age, Kellogg obtained an outfit and grubstake from two Murray residents, O. O. Peck, a contractor, and J. T. Cooper, a former British navy surgeon. Included in the grubstake was a mule. Legends are made from such strange and confused origins. It is doubtful that Kellogg's jackass discovered the vein of lead and silver as popular legend has recounted, but Kellogg somehow discovered a rich ledge and immediately staked two claims, giving himself one-half interest in both and his backers one-fourth. However, as the grizzled carpenter returned from the hills, his resentment against Peck and Cooper for their poor treatment of him grew. They had only invested seventeen dollars in the outfit and had, apparently, put Kellogg through a begging session to obtain that much. After this brooding, Kellogg decided to ignore his backers and instead engaged four new and trusted companions. When the five men reached Kellogg's original claim stakes, they tore them down, rubbed out the names, and transferred the stakes to two new locations. The famous Bunker Hill and Sullivan mines were thus born of dubious parentage.

As soon as the discovery became known, Peck and Cooper

retained lawyers and forced Kellogg into court in the attempt to recover interest in the rich strikes. The lawyers found a piece of paper on which, in Kellogg's handwriting, was the original description and claim to the Bunker Hill mine. During the suit, Kellogg steadfastly claimed that he had exhausted his meager grubstake before the mines were located. Although this meant that he would have consumed fifteen pounds of flour, ten pounds of beans, and thirty-five pounds of bacon in less than three days, the local jury believed him, in part because of their dislike for Peck and Cooper, and declared in Kellogg's favor. The territorial district judge, Norman Buck, overruled the jury because "their decision was contrary to evidence." Buck held that Kellogg was obligated to his original backers until the grub-stake was exhausted, and according to the judge, there was no way Kellogg, alone in the hills, could consume that much food in such a short time. Buck's decision was upheld as a case of clear fraud, and the Bunker Hill's ownership reverted to the original partnership.

A similar situation occurred when two other famous mines, the Emma and the Last Chance, less than a quarter of a mile from the holdings of Bunker Hill, were claimed. Charles Sweeny, a New York-born manipulator with national economic connections, bought the Emma and Last Chance lode claims in 1886. At one time or another, he controlled as many as sixty different mining claims. By the time Sweeny left the Coeur d'Alenes and settled in Spokane, Washington, he and his attorneys, especially Weldon B. Heyburn, a rotund, five-foot six-inch two-hundred-and-fifty pounder, had been in the courts almost continually for thirty years. Mining law was confusing, and Heyburn, who later became a United States senator from Idaho, tried to interpret it to Sweeny's advantage. The litigation involved with these claims eventually made its way to the United States Supreme Court. The basic issue revolved around the complexities of apex claims. Simplified, the question was: when the apex or an outcropping of a lode is discovered, does the original claim follow that lode underground even if the lode extends beyond the specified vertical limitation of the claim? In a number of court cases, Sweeny and his Last Chance Mine were finally victorious in getting a prior discovery ruling out of the Supreme Court. The court said that the first mine staked would have the rights to follow an underground lode even if it penetrated a neighbor's property. Many of the significant court battles between Sweeny and the Bunker Hill owners were finally resolved by merger, not by justice.

Railroads, merchants, gamblers, and saloons pushed rapidly into the Coeur d'Alene district. Lots sold for $2.50 in Wardner, the new town that resulted from Kellogg's discovery. In 1890, the population of Shoshone County was nearly four thousand and the miners that year extracted approximately ten million dollars worth of ore. The fabulous wealth in the mines brought into the area, as in the Wood River district, capitalists who could afford to develop the mines to full capacity.

Less than two years after the discovery of the Bunker Hill and Sullivan mines, Simeon G. Reed, the noted Portland businessman, paid an estimated $650,000 for the properties. Reed had already constructed a narrow-gauge railroad into most of the mining towns and gulches. Within four years, Reed disposed of the mines to a group of eastern capitalists. This pattern was followed throughout the district. Nearly all of the silver-lead mines discovered in the district were sold to eastern corporations by the time of Idaho's statehood. Although the mineowners fought among themselves and battled continually in the courts, their mineowners' association achieved some unity. Gigantic trusts were enveloping smaller companies, so without free competition, the mineowners had to organize in order to meet the smelter trust and the railroads on equal terms. In fact, at one time the mineowners closed the mines rather than pay a shipping increase to the railroads.

In 1899, J. P. Morgan brought eighteen companies together and organized the American Smelting and Refining Company. Two years later the massive Guggenheim interests consolidated with those of Morgan, and this trust controlled smelting in the United States and allotted lead production by district. Upset by the external control of the smelting trust that cut into their profits, most of the mine owners in the Coeur d'Alenes agreed to consolidate into the Federal Mining and Smelting Company in 1903. Charles Sweeny turned toward the East for the consolidation capital, and he found it in the fortunes of Jay Gould and John D. Rockefeller. Rockefeller sent his son, John D., Jr., to inspect personally the Coeur d'Alene mines, and when the negotiations ended, Federal poured ten million dollars into the consolidation.

Bunker Hill and Sullivan were able to avoid inclusion in the consolidated company because they owned their own smelters. By the time of Federal's consolidation, Bunker Hill had been sold to San Francisco bankers and Cyrus McCormick of International-Harvester. Interestingly, the Morgan, Guggenheim, Gould, Rockefeller, and McCormick millions were thus utilized to develop the Idaho mines. It is ironic to note that Sweeny attempted to purchase Bunker Hill in 1903, but the owners turned down Federal's offer. Thirteen years later, after an out-of-court settlement, Bunker Hill absorbed much of the Federal property. Bunker Hill and Sullivan survived the rapid exploitation of the 1890s and provided much of Idaho's lead-silver prosperity in the twentieth century. Also, activities at the Coeur d'Alene mines led to the bitter labor disputes of the 1890s and their baleful consequences: the intervention of federal troops, the incarceration of Populist party leaders, the murder of an ex-governor, and the resulting nationally famous trial. For some Americans the last decade of the nineteenth century might have been the "gay nineties," but for miners and mineowners in northern Idaho it was a period of strikes, bombings, and terror.

A union was initially organized in the Coeur d'Alene mines because Bunker Hill and Sullivan slashed the daily wages of miners from $3.50 to $3.00 and cut shovelers' pay from $3.50 to $2.50 per ten-hour day. The labor dispute issues usually revolved around wages, essential safety measures, and the living and buying conditions in the company town. Anytime there was a squeeze, wages were slashed and company prices skyrocketed. After a successful 1890–1891 strike, all of the underground wages were restored to $3.50 per day. As the unions organized to provide a rallying center for the miners, the owners became suspicious and vindictive. The Mine Owners' Protective Association was established, and they hired a Pinkerton detective, Charles Siringo, to infiltrate the union. Siringo, who worked in the mines as Leon Allison, was so successful that he served for seven months as the union recording secretary, while he regularly supplied the mineowners with the names of union organizers along with detailed plans of the union's proposed actions.

At the time the railroad companies raised their rates in 1891, and the mineowners responded by closing the mines, union men were left unemployed for the winter. After suffering profit losses, the owners determined to slash shoveler and carmen wages when the mines reopened. Union members were just as determined to strike for their $3.50. Faced by the possibility of a strike, the owners decided that a lockout would bring the miners around. Without work for many months and practically destitute, the Idaho miners received some relief in the form of $30,000 a month sent from Montana unions. The owners obtained a court injunction, which prohibited the strikers from trespassing, interfering with operations, or harassing any mine employees. Armed guards were recruited, and nonunion workers were hired to go into the mines.

Discouraged by their inability to win the strike, the union miners suddenly learned that Siringo was a company spy. The strikers reacted quickly with force and violence. A group of miners went to Gem and dynamited an abandoned mill, and in the ensuing fight, five men were killed. Another group seized three concentrators at Wardner and promised to blow them up if all nonunion workers were not dismissed immediately. The owners agreed to the demand and sent more than a hundred of the "scabs" to Lake Coeur d'Alene to await the arrival of a steamboat. While they were at the docks, another group of men, allegedly strikers, swept down upon the nonunion workers and robbed them.

Idaho's governor, Norman Willey, declared martial law and sent six companies of the Idaho National Guard into the Coeur d'Alenes, and they were joined by federal troops sent by President Benjamin Harrison. More than six hundred union leaders and sympathizers were arrested by the troops, and as many as three hundred and fifty were held in a large outdoor prison dubbed a "bullpen." Some of the leaders were taken to Ada County and others were shipped to Detroit, Michigan. By the spring of 1893, just as Grover Cleveland was taking office for a second time, the union leaders were freed. They had either served their terms or had their convictions reversed. In any event, they returned to the Coeur d'Alenes as heroes. It was while the union men were in jail that one of the attorneys, James Hawley, suggested to Ed Boyce, a local union leader, and others that the miners needed a union or federation that transcended specific mining district boundaries. Out of that suggestion and a variety of other forces, both the Western Federation of Miners and the Idaho Populist party were born.

Populism's hoped for alliance between miners and farmers was temporarily successful in Idaho. A plank of the Populist platform called for the free and unlimited coinage of silver, a plank that proved very popular in Idaho. Other planks, such as the nationalization of the monopolistic railroads and the direct election of senators, received Idaho endorsement to the point that Idaho's first electoral votes in 1892 went to the Populist candidate, Gen. James Weaver, and a Populist United States senator, Henry Heitfeld, and two Populist representatives, James Gunn and Thomas Glenn, were elected to Congress. Nearly seventy Populists were elected to the state legislature, including Ed Boyce, who had spent part of 1892 in jail. For Idaho miners, 1892 appeared to be the dawning of a bright new day. It was not to be so, as subsequent events in the Coeur d'Alenes illustrated.

The Western Federation of Miners was successful in persuading most of the mines to pay union scale wages throughout the 1890s, but the Bunker Hill and Sullivan owners successfully resisted. Secretly and slowly, the union began to enlist many Bunker Hill employees. Ed Boyce, now the WFM President, hoped to get enough Bunker Hill miners into the union ranks to call a successful strike against the giant mine. When Bunker Hill management found out about the union, they obtained membership lists and began to dismiss the union men. Union officials then threatened Bunker Hill employees and gave them the option either to join the union or leave town. Populist county officials joined with the governor, Frank Steunenberg, in calling for negotiations. Bunker Hill managers refused to arbitrate. They had fired all union members and would not talk to representatives of the union. Slowly the nonunion workers went back to work, and it appeared that the clever Bunker Hill management had thwarted the WFM again. The company hired a small army of guards and resumed normal operations.

Normality did not last long. On April 29, 1899, more than one hundred masked and armed miners commandeered a nine-car Northern Pacific train at Burke and forced the crew to drive it toward the Bunker Hill and Sullivan plant at Wardner. They stopped in Wallace and Kellogg and picked up hundreds of comrades and approximately three thousand pounds of dynamite. The Bunker Hill armed guards fled, as had the superintendent and manager. The miners burned the office and the bunkhouse. Methodically, they dynamited the large concentrator and blew the $250,000 plant out of existence. Numbering well over a thousand, the rebellious miners returned to the depot, fired guns in a five-minute celebration and let the train go.

All of the mines, except Bunker Hill and Sullivan, opened the next day, and the union members went about the business of mining. Their rejoicing was short-lived, however, for federal troops were already on their way to the Coeur d'Alene mines. Because the Idaho National Guard was involved in the Spanish-American War and was stationed in the Philippines, Governor Steunenberg obtained federal troops, under the command of Gen. H. C. Merriam, and martial law was declared. Many of the union participants fled to British Columbia or Montana, but hundreds of miners were gathered up and put in "bullpens," which consisted of two box cars, a wardhouse, and a two-story barn. Even the prolabor Populist sheriff, James Young, and the two Populist county commissioners were told to resign or go to jail. They ended up in a small jail cell. With the presence of the troops, the WFM was nearly forced out of existence. No one could work in the mines unless they signed an oath declaring that they did not belong to the WFM and that they had not participated in the bombings. James Hawley, who had earlier defended the miners, and William E. Borah prosecuted the case for the state. Because one man had been murdered, they decided to prosecute on charges of conspiracy.

Paul Corcoran, a union official from Burke, was eventually convicted of conspiracy, and ten other miners spent two years in federal prison for mail tampering. The Corcoran case presented some interesting aspects of the law. Corcoran's defense attempted to prove that the union official had not ridden the train that carried the laborers to Wardner and the dynamiting. Borah, who was prosecuting Corcoran for conspiracy, used the analogy that Corcoran was just as guilty as were the members of the Jesse James gang who stayed outside the bank and held the horses during a robbery. The defense tried to stick to the point that Corcoran was not at the scene of the crime and claimed that witnesses who reported seeing him sitting cross-legged on a railroad car with a rifle were in error. They argued that no one could sit that way and maintain his balance on the winding railroad, nor could an individual be recognized by onlookers. To prove the opposite, Borah dramatically rode the train for the jury's benefit—at the same rate of speed and sitting in the same position allegedly attributed to Corcoran. Martial law ended two years later, and the area returned to a state of peace. However, the suppression of the WFM in the Coeur d'Alenes gave rise to one more violent act of retribution that was to return Idaho's mining problems to the national news.

On a cold December night in 1905, former Governor Steunenberg, now a successful farmer and timberman in Caldwell, returned home late in the evening. As he opened the back gate, a bomb exploded, which killed him. Gov. Frank Gooding speculated that labor leaders had murdered Steunenberg because of the latter's use of federal troops in the Coeur d'Alene crisis six years earlier. Shortly thereafter, Harry Orchard, a miner using an alias, was arrested and held for the murder. Because evidence pointing to Orchard was scanty, Gooding arranged for James McParland, a celebrated antilabor Pinkerton detective, to come from Denver and investigate Orchard. The clever McParland, using a number of questionable techniques, obtained a sensational confession from Orchard after only their second meeting. Orchard not only admitted to the Steunenberg slaying, but also took credit for numerous Colorado dynamitings. According to Orchard's confession, these dynamitings had been planned and paid for by WFM officials headquartered in Denver.

McParland was now close to netting some elusive prey: William Haywood, the union's secretary, Charles Moyer, the president, and George Pettibone, a business associate of the union leaders, were named by Orchard as the men responsible for his activities. Haywood, a Utah-born agitator, had once been the secretary for the WFM local in Silver City. He was also a moving force in the 1905 organization of the Industrial Workers of the World. Even though the three WFM leaders were in Colorado at the time of Steunenberg's murder, McParland decided to have them charged with conspiracy. An extradition request was sent to Colorado officials by Governor Gooding, but McParland worried about the technicalities of the extradition proceedings. Knowing full well that a Colorado judge might release the three WFM officials on a technicality, McParland met with Colorado's governor and the chief justice, a man that Orchard claimed he once tried to dynamite. Convinced of the guilt of Haywood, Moyer, and Pettibone, the governor agreed to join McParland in carrying out an audacious plan. The three prisoners were loaded on a special Union Pacific train in Denver one Saturday morning, and by night, they were in Montpelier, Idaho. Heavily guarded, the train only stopped at remote stations for coal and water. The following day, the strange train arrived in Boise, and the three WFM leaders were deposited in the county jail. This was simply a kidnapping under the term "extradition." WFM attorneys were not successful in their attempt to prove that the "extradition" was also extralegal.

Idaho law required a corroborating witness, and this demand proved initially difficult and finally impossible for McParland. With reporters from all over the nation in Boise, the state proceeded with the testimony of Harry Orchard as the basis for its case against Moyer, Pettibone, and Big Bill Haywood. Haywood was tried first, and James Hawley, soon to be Idaho's governor, began the prosecution. He was joined by a somewhat reluctant William Borah, who was in the process of running for the U.S. Senate. Clarence Darrow came from the East to lead the Haywood defense. Since Orchard steadfastly stuck to his

story under a vicious Darrow cross-examination, Darrow resorted to a description of Orchard's sordid career, pointing out
that the jury was asked to believe a despicable confessed criminal. Since there was no corroborating evidence, in Darrow's
mind, there was no case. Borah tried to keep the issue of militant labor out of the trial, but asked the jury to reach a decision
on whether or not Haywood was guilty of conspiracy. Legally,
Darrow was right and the judge instructed the jury to find Haywood guilty only if Orchard's testimony could be corroborated.
The three WFM officials were acquitted, but Harry Orchard
served the last forty-nine years of his life in the cramped
quarters of the Idaho State Penitentiary. The Haywood case is
still an enduring mystery. Orchard stood by his story; yet Haywood and his associates remained free to follow an embittered
course that ultimately led Big Bill Haywood to the walls of the
Kremlin. Once freed, Haywood split with Moyer and the WFM
and became a leading IWW spokesman.

    Although the extradition procedures were questionable,
Idaho's courts did not make the mistakes that other states made
concerning the prosecution of labor activists. The atmosphere
was strained, but there was no capitulation to the economic
powers as was the case in the Chicago Haymarket Riot twenty
years earlier or the Joe Hill case in Utah a decade later. National
attention was focused on Idaho throughout the labor-
management struggles in the Coeur d'Alenes, which culminated
in the Haywood trial.

    With the Haywood case behind it, Idaho's labor difficulties
were minimized for some time, but unionization was now a definite reality. By the dawn of the twentieth century, the creation
of a political tradition, the establishment of a network of
railroads, and the consolidation of mineral interests converged
and the result was the state of Idaho. Although still sectionally
divided, the scene was now set for a concerted private, federal,
state, and local effort to control forest exploitation and reclaim
barren unproductive ground. Progressive measures designed to
guarantee agricultural prosperity and reserve forest acres make
a success story of impressive proportions.

6

Economic Lifeblood:
Water and Timber

$\mathcal{T}$UCKED away in the magnificent wilderness of central Idaho, surrounded by the Sawtooth, Boulder, White Cloud, and Salmon River mountains, is Stanley Basin, the headwaters of the Salmon River. Any of numerous small streams cascading down canyons to the valley floor are worthy of exploration. An amazing thing about this area is that the western foothills are all pine covered. The soft green hues of the valley meadows are contrasted to the darker pines, and both are set against the jagged snowcapped Sawtooths and the rich blue of the sky. The small creeks that feed the Salmon originate in the glaciers, springs, and lakes of the mountains. Their short journey to the mother river repeats in microcosm the Salmon's own raging rush through Idaho. Waterfalls and tiny rapids through the rocky slide areas are commonplace, but each is unique. As the icy clear water passes through the pine-covered foothills and nears the valley floor, it slows and can barely be heard. Along the trails an awesome awareness of the fragrance of pine and the presence of a virgin stream overcomes one. This is Idaho.

A similar description with regional variations fits the far eastern and northern parts of the state. The Snake River's Idaho origins are nearly as auspicious. Springs evolve into small streams and become creeks that merge into the mighty Snake. The pine-

115

and aspen-covered hills touch the banks of the rivers and reservoirs. Then there is northern Idaho where white pine reigns supreme. The entire drainage of the Clearwater River system is a magnificently forested, abundantly watered mountain paradise. Numerous small blue lakes as well as the beautiful large ones are richly endowed with a forested shoreline. Less water is used for irrigation in the north, but the real significance of Idaho is its water and its trees. How these resources were harnessed and harvested is an intricate part of Idaho's development.

Endowed with numerous verdant green stands of white pine, Douglas fir, and other softwoods, Idaho is one of the leading lumbering states in the nation. Two gigantic corporations, Boise Cascade and Potlatch Forests, base their operations in the forests of Idaho. Idaho timber interests ultimately came to enjoy considerable economic success, but not before a new era and new techniques came into being. Their rapid development in the early twentieth century is only surpassed by the simultaneous effort to bring water to the arid lands. Together, these two enterprises, timber and irrigated agriculture, are the basis upon which the Idaho economy succeeds or fails. It is an exciting story of individual ingenuity, governmental co-operation, reclamation, and conservation.

In 1900 a number of midwestern investors with previous timber experience pooled their resources and began moving into Idaho and the entire Pacific Northwest. The midwestern pine stands had been exploited, and the virgin forests of Idaho beckoned. One of the leading men in this movement was a very successful German immigrant, Frederick Weyerhaeuser. Joined by relatives, friends, and other businessmen, Weyerhaeuser made the decisions that led to the formation of many companies and a multimillion dollar business.

This combine ultimately purchased seven different Idaho ventures. Five of the seven were in the rugged mountains north of the Salmon River, and the other two were located south of the river in central Idaho. Weyerhaeuser and an associate, John Humbird, purchased forty thousand acres along the Clearwater River from the Northern Pacific Railroad. The expanding Wisconsin lumbermen also absorbed smaller companies and purchased large acreage along the Priest River, near Coeur d'Alene, beside the Kootenai River, and east of Moscow in the Palouse country. These lands were mostly acquired from the Northern Pacific, but the state of Idaho also sold some acres, as did private individuals and smaller companies. The Weyerhaeuser family, Edward Rutledge, and many other Wisconsin investors soon controlled considerable acreage north of the Salmon River. These five concerns temporarily were independent, but the forces of economic necessity eventually drove them together.

Wisconsin-owned firms, with Weyerhaeuser connections, also bought some state and independently owned lands in the Boise and Payette River drainage after 1902. In 1903, Potlatch Lumber Company, a concern based in Maine, had bought heavily into the northern and central Idaho tree country. The Barber Lumber Company secured twenty-five thousand acres of timberland on tributaries of the Boise River from former Gov. Frank Steunenberg. The other corporation, the Payette Lumber and Manufacturing Company, took over some state-owned lands in the Payette Basin that the organizers of the Potlatch Forest Company had originally purchased. The new president of this enterprise, William Musser, was related to the directors of most of the Panhandle lumber companies.

The northern companies had ready access to railroads and were able to construct rail feeder lines or use the streams in order to move the logs to a sawmill. In the mountains northeast of Boise, it was a much more difficult and demanding task. Because there were no railroads and because the Ponderosa pine did not survive water transportation well, the companies floundered. Another factor that hindered their attempt to exploit the timber on the public domain was an 1878 federal law which stated that federally owned land could only be acquired in 160-acre tracts. Since 160-acre farms were proving inadequate for western homesteaders, family-size timber holdings were actually even worse. A number of family-owned sawmills just could not compete with the new giant corporations. However, many opportunistic individuals took advantage of the federal law by claiming land, and as soon as the deed was granted, they would

sell the acres to one of the big companies. After lengthy litigation, sympathetic federal judges allowed the companies to consolidate purchases in excess of the 160 acres.

Ironically, all of this purchasing, consolidating, and organizing was taking place while Theodore Roosevelt and Gifford
Pinchot were fighting to create a national forest system that
would guarantee conservation. Idaho's senators were often split
over this issue, and Fred Dubois, the Mormon-baiter, voted
with Roosevelt, while Weldon Heyburn, the north Idaho anti-
union lawyer, opposed Roosevelt's plans vociferously. By
1906, Roosevelt had, through executive order, withdrawn most
of the unappropriated national timberlands from exploitation and
called them national forests. Senator Heyburn led a successful
congressional fight that forbade the president from enlarging the
national forest without congressional consent. The president,
with the concurrence of Pinchot and other advisers, then added
all the lands to the national forest that the forest service deemed
desirable, before he signed the bill. Idaho's Senator Heyburn,
irate over Roosevelt's action, exerted his influence to persuade
Congress to withhold operating funds from the Forest Service.
Without the proper and necessary budget, the service thus had
to curtail many of its activities and programs. Included among
those services hampered was adequate fire protection for the national forests.

Although the state had joined the lumber companies to form
regional fire protection associations, these proved dramatically
ineffective during the great burn of 1910. Before it was finally
contained, one-sixth of the national forest land of northern
Idaho was burned, and generations would pass before those
mountains were again tree-covered. As if to demonstrate to
Heyburn the short-sightedness of his vindictive policies, a third
of his hometown, Wallace, was burned before the fireline finally held. It is probable that no amount of 1910-vintage fire
protection could have saved northern Idaho from the destruction
of that year, but the fire taught the nation a lesson concerning
the need for a decent and competent fire prevention and detec-
tion system. After the 1910 burn left a charred and stark re-

minder of what might have been prevented, the Forest Service received the needed funds.

Even with accessible railroads and available rivers, early commercial lumbering did not return easy profits for the midwestern investors. Anticipating control of the eastern market because of their accessibility to railroads, Weyerhaeuser and his associates miscalculated badly. The timbermen had believed that the southern United States softwood forests would soon be depleted and that the cost of shipping Pacific Coast wood eastward would be prohibitive. They figured that Idaho lumber would fill the vacuum. Nature proved them wrong concerning southern timber, and the activities of man destroyed their calculations concerning expensive Washington and Oregon wood. The climate and moisture in the south caused forests to reproduce at a much higher rate than had been anticipated; and the completion of the Panama Canal made it possible for Pacific Coast timber to be shipped to the East Coast by boat cheaper than it could be obtained from Idaho by rail. In fact, wood could be shipped for less via Panama and eastern railroads to Cleveland, Ohio, than it could from Coeur d'Alene to Cleveland. With permanent competition from the South and the West Coast, there was no ready market for all of the Idaho timber, and thus Idaho timberlands were not completely cut out as they were in the Great Lakes. In a sense, Idaho's forests were saved by Theodore Roosevelt's acquisition of Panama and the resultant construction of the Panama Canal. Still, the timber industry surpassed mining in its importance to Idaho's economy. It was not until World War II that there were unlimited demands for Idaho timber, but by then most of the original small companies had merged into either Potlatch Forests in the north or Boise Payette, later Boise Cascade, in the south.

It is a fact that Idaho timber never returned the quick profit that investors, managers, and outside observers anticipated. Just as the mountains of Idaho had proved inhospitable to explorers, trappers, and missionaries, timbermen found that the new environment dictated a change in the lumberman's game rules. Initially, the industry's economics left no alternative but to clear

cut and then get out. So long as timber was there, the philosophy was to get it before someone else did and then plow the
profits into the next venture. In a similar way, the timber industry was analogous to the old trapping business. It was immediately opportunistic and placed a premium on exploitation.
Once the trees were felled, then the idea was to get rid of the
land as soon as possible in order to avoid continued taxes on
used timberland. It was not uncommon to relinquish the land
back to the government in lieu of paying the taxes. No thought
was given to using the land to develop a new stand of timber.
That would take time, and lumbermen believed that patience
was not a virtue in their business. The passage of time and different management would alter that perception.

Of the original seven major companies, only one, that managed by Thomas Humbird in far northern Idaho, showed a
profit. Humbird, the son of the original Weyerhaeuser partner,
practiced a policy of clear cutting with no plans for reforestation. Using Lake Pend Oreille as a storage area and buying
wisely, Humbird was able to produce more than two billion
board feet of lumber before liquidating the entire project in the
late 1930s. The Weyerhaeuser family closed their Bonners Ferry
Operation in 1926 after pouring more than a million dollars of
loans into it. No dividends were ever sent to the stockholders;
and floods, fires, rate differentials, and international confusions
over Canadian timber conspired to destroy the operation.

The Rutledge, Clearwater, and Potlatch firms eventually
merged into Potlatch Forests Incorporated during the midst of
the Great Depression. The Rutledge Company had long-term
debts in excess of $4 million and had not produced dividends
for thirty years at the time of the merger. Even with the most
modern equipment and a new railroad line, the Clearwater Company had debts of over $2 million by 1930. Even the Potlatch
Company had very rough sledding during the first three decades
of competition. It was a fact of national economic life that Idaho
lumber could not compete in price on the national market.
Rough terrain, high transportation costs, and a smaller volume
of timber per acre combined to force the price upward.

The Potlatch enterprise was saved by some far-sighted policies adopted by state and company officials. For one thing, the Idaho legislature enacted a tax law that not only lowered the property tax on harvested lands, but also on lands placed in reproduction. G. F. ("Fritz") Jewett and E. C. Rettig, company employees, and David Mason, a consultant, were instrumental in creating an atmosphere for treating trees as a crop, not as a single, once-only product. The adoption of this concept led to a policy of selective cutting, reforestation, and the development of sustained yield in Idaho's forests.

It took a long time for the far-sighted conservation policies formulated to pay off in stockholders' dividends. C. L. Billings, a blunt and aggressive leader, was determined to make conservation a basic company policy. In order to wait patiently for tree farms to produce and for company-owned lands to develop, it was necessary to go elsewhere for trees, and Billings went to his former employers, the United States Forest Service. By cooperating with state and federal officials, Billings was able to lease government lands to the degree that a sustained yield could be maintained while reforestation ran its course. Yet, it was still World War II before PFI began to pay annual dividends to its stockholders. After the war, consumer demand intensified, and the products an "instant" society requires—paper plates, napkins, and milk cartons—led to the expansion of PFI into a number of tree-related industries outside of lumber and plyboard.

A similar story occurred in south central Idaho. Although the Barber and Payette companies had secured thousands of acres of heavily forested land, the companies simply did not pay dividends. Even after a merger was completed on the eve of World War I, Boise Payette, the new company, still had difficulties. After deciding that they could not compete in the eastern market, the managers opened a number of retail outlets throughout the intermountain area. While manufacturing remained in the red, the retail outlets provided the profits to keep the new company afloat during the 1920s. This company had always followed the "clear cut" and then "get out" policy, so the depression and the disappearance of trees on their land ended prosperity in the 1930s. Under the leadership of E. P. Clapp, a trained physician, and Jack Moon, an experienced lumberman, Boise Payette retrenched throughout the 1930s. Retail yards were closed, mills sawed their last timber, and a company-owned railroad ceased operation. Of course, these policies resulted in increased unemployment which contributed to the depression cycle. Inaccessible timberland was traded to the Forest Service for accessible acres. Slowly the company regained its feet and began to discuss expansion. But the manufacturing phase of Boise Payette was endangered because the trees were about gone. Expansion of the retail outlets was effected after World War II, but the clear cut policy had left the company with no more timberlands.

New leaders, especially John Aram, a stocky University of Idaho product, developed a plan to save Boise Payette's manufacturing and timber activities and prepare the company for a permanent existence in Idaho. It was proposed, just as Potlatch had done, that timber be purchased from the Forest Service while the company-owned cutover lands were prepared for reproduction. While the young trees were developing, the lands could be leased to cattlemen's associations for grazing pasture. Within a short time, Boise Payette, like Potlatch Forests, was treating timber as a crop. Advanced forestry principles were utilized, and tree farms were certified on Boise Payette lands. Like PFI, the company prospered during the 1950s and attracted more managerial types, such as Robert V. Hansberger. The name of the corporation was changed to Boise Cascade, and diversification and expansion made Boise Cascade almost a conglomerate. In fact, during the 1960s, they expanded too rapidly in many directions and suffered the economic consequences.

Both companies still depend on the vast forests of Idaho for much of their corporate prosperity. However, PFI and Boise Cascade are heavily involved in other states and around the world. Much of the actual logging and milling is handled by smaller subcontractors. The tree crops are not perennials, and it will take a long time for the company-owned lands to produce the lumber demanded by the consuming public. Consequently, the companies still request favors from the national forest. More and more, they are seeking to exploit and log forests in the

Idaho Primitive Area or in national forest acreage previously denied. The ecological damage done by modern logging techniques of cables, diesel-powered cat tractors, and blasting will take generations to repair. Although jobs are created, taxes are paid, timber provided, and growth stimulated by the timber industry, careful forest management is an absolute necessity if Idaho's green-timbered mountains are to stand as a symbol for an appreciation of nature's magnificence.

However, timber viewed as a crop puts trees in the same agricultural category as potatoes, wheat, alfalfa, and sugar beets. Since the Forest Service is in the Department of Agriculture, that concept is not totally ludicrous. Farming is the primary industry of Idaho, and successful production depends on the availability and distribution of water.

When a traveler passes through the Snake River valley of south central Idaho, he is struck by the apparent agricultural prosperity. Field after field of row crops and grain receive a dousing from the highly mechanized sprinkler systems. Moving slowly across the fields, these long, strange-looking devices provide an almost certain guarantee for a heavy production. A vast system of canals slices through the Snake River Plain, and many small farmers, unable to purchase the expensive sprinklers, still flood their land by opening a headgate and allowing the water to penetrate the rows in numerous tiny streams. This farming paradise, with its deep rich volcanic-ash topsoil, was, for most of Idaho's history, an uninviting, dry, desolate, sagebrush plain. Its prosperity and settlement, for the most part, is of twentieth-century vintage and is one of the most remarkable stories of land reclamation in American history.

Thousands of westward-moving pioneers passed through the semiarid valley without any desire to stop, plant crops, and settle. The well-watered verdant valleys of Oregon and California, with their more moderate climates, beckoned. These pioneers realized by intuition and observation what the U. S. Weather Bureau could document with statistics at a later date—that an average annual rainfall of ten to twelve inches just does not make farming possible without irrigation. But as cheap and free western land gradually disappeared, land-hungry pioneers would find ways to use the many tributaries of the Snake River, as well as the mighty stream itself, to put water on the land.

Idaho irrigation began with Henry H. Spalding, the missionary at Lapwai, who dug a ditch from the Clearwater River in order to get water onto his dying garden. The real beginnings of reclamation irrigation in Idaho came with the Mormons when they settled the Lemhi, Cache, Bear Lake, and Malad valleys in Idaho, and with the first farmers who stayed in the Boise valley. For twenty years, the Mormons applied co-operation and communal efforts to build the earliest pioneer canal systems. Because of the aridity, the Mormons developed an entirely different concept of water law that ultimately became the legal basis for water utilization in Idaho.

Heretofore, the English common law doctrine of riparian rights had been used. Riparian rights held that the landholder whose lands were adjacent to a stream was entitled to as much of the stream's water as he desired. Without adequate rainfall (and it was not adequate in many western states) this meant that only lands next to waterways could be successfully developed. Consequently, a new law based on "prior appropriation" was developed. This meant that a farmer or a group of farmers could divert and use water from a stream without reference to ownership of adjoining land, provided that their use did not interfere with earlier similar use. A priority sequence coupled with an amount, usually in usable hours, of appropriation was developed. As the law of appropriation developed, a system of filing for water was defined. A farmer could apply for the amount of water that was needed for his land. The land was usually in tracts of 160 acres because of the Homestead Act provisions, but after passage of the 1877 Desert Land Act, a family might acquire an entire 640-acre section.

In a series of court decisions, the Idaho Supreme Court upheld the idea of prior appropriation and gave it superiority over the riparian rights doctrine. In fact, the Idaho State Constitution confirmed the tenet that the water belonged to the state, and all future applications for appropriation had to be made through the state. State law also sets priorities for Idaho water usage, with domestic needs primary, followed by agriculture, and manufacturing last. If a farmer or a manufacturer is found guilty of wasting water, it is a misdemeanor. Since so much of the early irrigation in southeastern Idaho began prior to the formulation of Idaho law, numerous legal tangles evolved. Wisely, the state created the concept of the irrigation district, which enabled land owners to organize, construct canals and dams, and supervise the distribution of the water. However, many fights in and out of courtrooms, and some deaths, have been caused by disputes over water. In the eyes of many farmers, especially during dry years, water thievery is a crime second only to murder.

Irrigation in the Boise River valley was completely different from that of the upper Snake River and Magic valleys. A different kind of irrigation economics was applied in the Boise area, and the results were of consequence. Almost simultaneous with the gold rush into the Boise Basin during the mid-1860s was an influx of farmers who settled along the banks of the Boise River. Small groups of farmers co-operated in an attempt to bring more water to the potentially productive acres. In eastern Idaho, Mormons, already organized for community co-operation, had completed this task, but in the Boise area it was left to private canal companies to develop the canals and ditches. One of the most interesting operations was that undertaken by the Idaho Mining and Irrigation Company. Prompted by the coming of the Oregon Short Line, New York investors poured capital into the construction of the New York Canal. Their goal was to provide irrigation water to the bench areas around Boise. It was hoped that the project could be paid for by using the excess water to work placer mines along the Snake River. Fine gold was there, but the economics of location and production were out of sight. Even if the mining aspect did not work out, the New York Canal still had great potential for success. The railroad could bring farmers into the reclaimed area and, at the same time, guarantee an eastern market for their crops. From its inception, the New York Canal was a grand and complicated endeavor.

In the early 1880s, a number of New Yorkers came to Boise and began filing claims on Boise River water. John H. Burns initially claimed more water than the river carried during its peak. Burns anticipated bringing water out of the Boise River about ten miles upstream from the city and diverting it into two canals that would move toward the eastern and western ends of the valley. Other New Yorkers arrived in 1883 to survey the land and prepare for the ditch construction. One of these later arrivals was the company engineer, A. D. Foote, who contemplated the construction of a seventy-five-mile main canal and more than five thousand miles of lateral ditches. Foote visualized that eventually nearly a half million acres of arid land could be brought under cultivation if his seventeen-foot-deep, twenty-seven-foot-wide ditch could be completed. Until a large impoundment was completed, there was no way Foote's expectations would have reached fulfillment.

On the basis of talk and promotion, homesteaders started to move on to the lands west of Boise. If that canal worked, they could prove up on their land in two or three years instead of the five required by the homestead law. However, it cost enormous amounts of money to build a canal down from a canyon, and the construction moved slowly and at times actually halted. Because the New York Canal construction was moving so slowly, a pair of Philadelphia-based businessmen, James Stewart and James A. McGee, obtained an option to complete the west end of the grandiose canal system. Naming their canal Phyllis, after McGee's daughter, they hired some men and set about to bring Boise River water into the Nampa area. As with the New York Canal, the Phyllis simply could not be finished because of engineering problems and the lack of funds. Although the Idaho Central Railway tried to buy the Phyllis Canal, the owners refused to sell, and allowed the Idaho Mining and Irrigation Company to re-establish control over both the New York and Phyllis claims. So after nearly seven years of promoting, advertising, and digging, no real water was running through the proposed canals of the Boise valley.

In 1890, faced with bankruptcy and hurting from charges of fraud, the Idaho Mining and Irrigation Company signed a contract with W. C. Bradbury's Denver-based construction company. For over a year, Bradbury kept between two and five hundred men working on the canals, mostly the Phyllis. By the growing season of 1891, water was running thirty-five miles to the Nampa area and providing the promised respite from aridity. The water also provided an opportunity for some to try to find gold on the Snake River, but that endeavor was of little significance compared to the bringing of water to the farm ground west of Boise.

Bradbury, who was personally in charge, attempted to complete the difficult New York Canal. Faced by a seemingly insurmountable problem of cutting a canal down miles of canyon, but persistent and tenacious, he pushed on even after British and American bondholders withdrew their funding of the Idaho Mining and Irrigation Company that had hired him. Finally, Bradbury, too, ran out of funds. Before he quit, exhausted and discouraged, nearly $400,000 had been poured into the New York Canal project. Over half of it was money from his own funds. The canal through the canyon was unfinished, so the remainder of the fourteen miles under construction could not get water anyway. Angry over his losses, in 1894 Bradbury hired William E. Borah as legal counsel. Borah was successful in obtaining both canals from the defunct Idaho Mining and Irrigation Company for $184,000 at an Ada County sheriff's sale.

It was 1900 before water was turned into the New York Canal, and by then Foote, Bradbury, and the rest of the early developers were out of the picture. Two different competing groups finished the canal's construction. Finally, the New York Canal Company was organized by Charles Fifer, whose shareholders were appropriated water in proportion to the number of shares they owned. Assisted by federal funds authorized under the 1902 Reclamation Act, a canal system was finally completed. The finished product was a strange canal that would only carry 300 second feet of water through the canyon, but the next six miles of the canal was the large ditch envisioned by Foote, which could carry up to 2,200 second feet. Then it narrowed to a ditch as small as the one in the canyon. By 1906 only 38,000 acres were open to irrigation—a far cry from the grandiose schemes of A. D. Foote. The U. S. Reclamation Service took over the project and enlarged the canals and constructed diversion dams.

Private enterprise and competition proved inadequate to solve the needs of the Boise area. Years of litigation, confusion, and excessive distribution of nonexistent water were finally solved by the realization that the real problem was water shortage. A climate was created by the troubles that made a federal reclamation role not only accepted but applauded. The Lucky Peak, Arrowrock, and Anderson Ranch dams, and the entire federally supported Boise Project accomplished for the state capital area what New York and Philadelphia investors could not—a workable system of reservoirs and canals that could provide water to parched soil during the hot summer days of August.

Fortunately for Idaho, projects in other areas proved more successful.

They call it Idaho Irrigation District Thirty-Six. It stretches from spectacular Jackson Lake in Wyoming all the way to the beautiful Hagerman Valley in south central Idaho. The nearly three-hundred-mile-long district is governed by nine representatives of each of the major sections of irrigation along the Snake River. When the numerous tributary projects are added to the major Snake system, the water district supervises thousands of miles of streams that irrigate millions of acres. This sample of irrigation democracy, perhaps the largest in the nation, still survives. It is a clear example of how federal, state, local, and private co-operation was necessary to turn the sagebrush-covered Snake River Plain into a vast Idaho garden. There were numerous setbacks and continued difficulties; yet co-operation and patience prevailed. It was the massive utilization of Snake River water that pushed agriculture products beyond minerals and timber to become Idaho's most important economic asset.

Since most of the naturally well-watered land in the country had been claimed by the end of the Civil War, extensive settlement in the West depended on bringing water to the new land. In the decades following the Civil War, most land laws were only marginally successful in prompting farmers to homestead. As a rule, the land laws passed between 1865 and the twentieth century were similar in two regards. In the first place, all the laws were easily used by speculators, land companies, and corporations. Consequently, most acres were purchased from railroads, state governments, and land companies. Secondly, the laws were unrealistic for the needs of farmers in the arid West. The physical requirements were so drastically different that a 160-acre homestead was too small for stock raising and too large for a single family irrigation unit. The Desert Land Act of 1877 granted 640 acres, a full section, but it required that it be under irrigation within three years. The expense involved was prohibitive to a single family. As Sen. William E. Borah stated, "the government bets 160 acres against the entry fee of $14 that the settler can't live on the land for five years without starving to death." [1] Although these laws were altered to allow for filing on fewer acres, they were not successful in enticing farmers onto the desert lands. They were important, however, in paving the way for future developments.

In 1894, Wyoming Sen. Joseph M. Carey proposed a bill that would provide for the cession of a million acres of federal land to any western state that would be willing to reclaim the acres. The land could be sold in parcels as small as forty acres, but at least forty acres had to be brought under irrigation. At that point, the settler could obtain a patent on the land. Later amendments stipulated that the state could have a lien on the land to protect private capital and that the state and investors had ten years to complete the irrigation project after they commenced construction. The construction company sold water rights to the individual farmer, and the state sold the land for fifty cents an acre, with half the money down and the remainder when final proof was made. When the irrigation system was completed, the contract between the state and the construction company stipulated that the water share owners would operate the system. The state had full responsibility to fund, plan, and supervise the disposal of Carey Act lands. Apparently, most states were reluctant to take advantage of the Carey Act provisions, but Idaho was

1. William D. Gertsch, "The Upper Snake River Project: A Historical Study of Reclamation and Regional Development, 1890–1930" (Ph.D. dissertation, University of Washington, 1974), p. 118.

not, and the Twin Falls project became the national showcase
for the success of the Carey Act.

In order to bring water to Idaho's Magic valley, numerous individuals from around the nation combined their talents and fortunes. Frank Riblett, a pioneer surveyor, John Hayes, an engineer, and John Hansen, a farmer, early dreamed of a vast
irrigation system and reservoir storage areas throughout the
Snake River valley, but they lacked capital. John Wesley Powell,
the noted surveyor and explorer, had always believed water
could make the Snake River valley productive. Even though
some farmers filed appropriation notices and surveyed their
canal lines, the depression-riddled 1890s was not the time to get
money. Ira B. Perrine, an Indiana-born Idaho settler, took up
the work of the early surveyors and was able to combine Idaho,
Illinois, and Pennsylvania financial interests in a way to bring
water to the Twin Falls area.

In 1900, Perrine persuaded Stanley Milner, a wealthy Salt
Lake City businessman, to invest $30,000 in a survey for the
project. After some initial financial setbacks, they luckily prevailed upon a mining broker, Witcher Jones, to join them. Jones
represented several wealthy eastern industrialists who had invested in western mines, and Jones sold them on the idea of
canal construction. Frank H. Buhl, a steel millionaire from
Sharon, Pennsylvania, came to Idaho, and Perrine hurried him
around the Magic valley in a number of horsedrawn wagons.
Buhl returned to the East, and with the help of his associate,
Peter Kimberly, secured bond issues from a Chicago bonding
house.

All of these financial maneuvers consumed the better part of
three years. Finally, in 1903, Idaho contracted with the Twin
Falls Land and Water Company, the official name of the Per-
rine-Buhl-Kimberly combine, to develop more than a quarter of
a million acres under Carey Act provisions. The state sold the
land and the company sold the water; so both agencies saw immediate benefits. The terrain over which the canals traversed
was not especially rugged or difficult. By 1905 a diversion
dam, named for Milner, on the Snake was completed and a
major canal, ten feet deep and eighty feet wide, was carrying

water to sixty thousand acres of farmland south of the Snake River. One of the nation's largest irrigation projects was underway. Perrine's dogged persistence paid off because it took the actual sight of water going down the canal to sell the land. Buhl, Kimberly, and their general manager, Walter Filer, had almost withdrawn their support after the initial land sale only attracted about a dozen people. But by the end of 1905, Twin Falls was literally an agricultural boom town. Eventually the entire 270,000 acres allotted by the state to the company was sold, and Buhl prospered accordingly.

Buhl was not interested when Perrine asked him to finance a project north of the Snake. Perrine persuaded the Kuhn family of Pittsburgh to join him in development north of the river. Although a large tract was ultimately sold, which also obtained water from the Milner Dam, Perrine and the Kuhns faced a number of significant problems. One of their contemplated storage reservoirs would not fill because of the porous soil, and they sold more land than they could supply with water. Thus, during dry years when the need for water on the upper Snake was high, the farmers of Jerome and Wendell went without. There was no guarantee that water would be always available, and this fact led to the failure of many Carey Act projects. It was not until the federal government intervened and the huge management district was organized that water in August could be a surety.

The Kuhn interests also involved themselves in Carey Act projects on Salmon Falls Creek southwest of Twin Falls and near Oakley, south of Milner Dam. In the Salmon Falls tract they oversold and were never able to deliver water to all of the acres they had promised. During a depression in 1913, the vast Kuhn holdings, which included railroad, coal, and banks, went into the hands of receivers. However, the north side project was completed after Perrine persuaded the government to increase the holding capacity of Jackson Lake.

Although hundreds of thousands of Idaho acres were brought under irrigated cultivation through the provisions of the Carey Act, not all projects enjoyed the enormous success of the Twin Falls projects. These farmers took over the operation of the canals and continued to work for better control and more positive assurance of water. The state had to involve itself in troubled Carey Act projects near King Hill below Twin Falls, the one on Salmon Falls Creek, and the Big Lost River project near Arco. Gov. Moses Alexander, a German-born immigrant to Idaho, was the moving force behind the progressive attempt to assist farmers who were cheated by overspeculation. Alexander was instrumental in seeing every Carey Act project organized into an irrigation district. He also proposed that the state pay the court costs for any settler who sued the construction company when it failed to deliver the needed and promised water. In these proposals, Alexander was doing precisely what U. S. Reclamation Service head, Fred Newell, suggested. Newell believed that the states needed to play an active role in the Carey Act reclamation projects, and one method he proposed was for the state and the federal government to use matching funds in order to preserve faltering Carey Act projects.

What the Carey Act experience taught Idahoans was that in order to guarantee needed water, a greater system of organization had to be perfected and that the federal government should be used to reach that goal. Ira Perrine and his associates had succeeded in one respect; yet the problems faced by water users were still enormous.

With his stewardship theory of government, Theodore Roosevelt was attracted to the idea of federal sponsorship of reclamation projects. Although his national forest policies were opposed by most western politicians, his ideas concerning land reclamation received considerable support. The president was convinced by the logic of Nevada Sen. Francis Newlands that there were many needed irrigation projects that were simply too expensive and complicated to be funded by private capital or state money. The resultant legislation, the National Reclamation Act, or Newlands Act, provided that the monies obtained from the sale of western lands be used to fund irrigation systems for the arid areas. The legislation passed by Congress in 1902 has had an enduring impact in Idaho. The Bureau of Reclamation has constructed a number of projects, including the Minidoka, American Falls, and Palisades dams along the Snake and the entire

Payette-Boise system in western Idaho. It also sold storage rights in the various reservoirs to canal companies and needy irrigation districts.

One of the initial Newlands projects was the Minidoka Dam about thirty-five miles upstream from the Milner Dam. Work on the dam was started in 1904, less than two months before Roosevelt won the presidency in his own right. Water was eventually diverted on both the north and south sides of the river, and well in excess of one hundred thousand acres was opened to farmers. The northern canal was suited for gravity flow, but the south side system that serviced Burley had to have a series of pumping stations in order to move the water where it was needed. There was often a severe shortage of water and funds to keep the south side operating. These shortages compounded the problems of settlers farther down the river and led to the demand for greater storage facilities upriver. The Minidoka Project ultimately cost in excess of six million dollars, but provided canals, storage, and electrical power. The power was originally produced for the purpose of pumping irrigation water into areas where gravity flow was impossible. With surplus power generated by the Minidoka Dam, a local distribution system was established. This early success in developing a federal power project proved a useful argument for George Norris during his persistent campaign to get the TVA bill through Congress.

Simultaneous with the construction of the Minidoka Dam, the Bureau of Reclamation was in the process of constructing a timber crib dam on Jackson Lake in Wyoming. When the first stage of the project was finished, the water level had risen fifteen feet, and many smaller natural lakes had become the larger Jackson Lake. As a temporary measure, the reclamation people believed that Jackson Lake could control the flow of the Snake until a larger dam was built that would eventually triple the amount of water impounded. As soon as the project was completed, thirsty downstream irrigation units, such as the Twin Falls north side company, were negotiating for federal water. Resentment against federal participation in an area previously reserved for private capital dissipated as the scorched earth swallowed the liquid treasure. It was necessary for the canal companies to use federal water in order to survive during droughts, which seemed to occur about every five years. However, the organization of a system for use of the Snake River was becoming unbelievably complicated. During times when Jackson Lake water was released to aid the Minidoka project, all of the upper Snake customers were forbidden use of the water and were instructed to keep their headgates closed. Understandably, vicious disputes arose and on occasion violence was the result. After the severe drought of 1919, in which fifteen million dollars worth of crops were lost, distrust over distribution and allocation reached a peak. For example, if the Snake River was nearly dry at Blackfoot, one hundred miles above the Minidoka Dam, and water was released from Jackson Lake for Magic valley use, the Blackfoot farmers refused to close the headgates and the coveted water never arrived in south central Idaho. Of course, lower valley residents felt those in the upper valley were either holding back or overusing. Out of this spirit of distrust, coupled with the horrendous economic setbacks of 1919, some leadership finally evolved which ultimately settled many of the Snake River valley disputes.

By 1920 there were thirty different irrigation districts and over forty separate companies competing for use of the Snake River. From the Wyoming border to points below Twin Falls, over three hundred miles, the life-giving water was the center of controversy. Organization and co-operation were essential if the irrigation system were to survive. Out of this atmosphere of crisis, the Idaho Reclamation Association was born in Pocatello in 1919. Many local groups had already banded together and moved toward co-operation. Fred Reed, the association secretary, envisioned a large district for the entire valley, but he was also interested in expanding projects to open more land. Others wanted to control existing water before they spread it more thinly on new dry acres.

The state engineer in 1919 called a meeting in Idaho Falls, at which he selected a committee of nine men from all parts of the Snake River valley, to devise an acceptable plan for water distribution. For four years, this committee met and discussed the mammoth problems of the entire irrigation district. In 1923, the formal Committee of Nine was established, and each representative was elected by the farmers of the specified area. District Thirty-Six—some claim it is the largest irrigation district in the world—was created the next year as a working example of irrigation democracy. As a consequence of the committee's activities and recommendations, past difficulties were understood, if not solved, and future needs were approached with basic enlightened unity.

One thing the committee did was to convince farmers that the normal flow of the Snake River had been overextended because of the continual opening of new projects. A hired Colorado engineer, F. T. Meeker, also convinced the committee that Minidoka and Jackson Lake reservoirs were inadequate for the present needs of the full valley, let alone the future demands. Meeker proposed that more storage facilities be constructed as an ironclad guarantee that water would be available year around. The accuracy of Meeker's report, the success of the Committee of Nine, and irrigation co-operation was attested to the next year, 1924, when the lower valley was plagued by another severe water shortage. Russell Shepherd, a native New Yorker and a committee representative, proposed that other members appeal to users in the upper valley with prior rights to donate water to fellow farmers near Twin Falls. As a result of the willing response to the appeal, mature crops developed in the Magic valley. Once again, the need for more reservoirs was dramatically documented by nature's erratic behavior.

American Falls had been picked as a possible damsite by nearly every engineer who surveyed the Snake River prior to the 1920s. It was not just a simple matter of building a dam because the entire town of American Falls had to be relocated—lands had to be purchased from the Shoshoni-Bannock Fort Hall Reservation, three miles of Union Pacific track had to be rebuilt, and a million-dollar arrangement had to be made with the Idaho Power Company, which operated a generator at the base of the falls. Warren G. Harding had campaigned as a friend of western reclamation and once elected, he tried to find out what projects were feasible and how others were functioning. He dispatched his new interior secretary to the West on a fact-finding mission.

After Secretary Albert B. Fall came to Idaho in 1921 and surveyed the projected American Falls damsite and reservoir, he attempted to curtail the federal funding. Since Idaho farmers on the Minidoka project were delinquent on their payments to the government, Fall could not see much sense in expanding the federal role, even if the Bureau of Reclamation wanted to build a new dam. For nearly a year the project was held in virtual limbo. The Idaho congressional delegation, led by Senator Borah, combined with Gov. D. W. Davis, the Committee of Nine, Idaho Power, and the farmers tried to convince Fall that the farmers, Idaho Power, and the state would guarantee the success of the American Falls venture. All of the materials were placed on Fall's desk, but the secretary, who was apparently more interested in cattle and oil, went to Texas with Edward Doheny for six weeks and refused to act on the Idaho proposal. When Fall finally returned to Washington in February of 1923, his old Senate colleague, William Borah, was waiting. Borah presented the concept of the single irrigation district to Fall, and the secretary promised federal funds if the local people could raise a share of the money.

Because of the unified appearance, six bond bidders tried for the $2.7 million American Falls contract. Amazingly, the locally operated irrigation district was considered solvent enough to guarantee the bonds. Ultimately, over $8 million was used to construct the mammoth mile-wide dam, move the town, rebuild the railroad, and put the system in operation by 1927. Nearly two million acre feet of water is impounded by the twenty-five-mile-long reservoir. The irrigation aspect of the project successfully provided water directly or by exchange to a million acres of land and guaranteed a water supply for all of the existing projects in the Magic valley.

The American Falls Dam is important in the development of Idaho and the West for another significant reason. Success on this unique and trying agrarian frontier was furnished by a genuine concept of co-operation and community. Very few rugged individualistic frontier farmers survived without the assistance of outside capital and the crutch of the federal government. Success at American Falls was not only because of federal tax dollars, but because the individual users were clever enough to organize, submerge their differences, and work for the common good. Private capital and public monies were brought to bear with positive results.

The only losers at American Falls were the Fort Hall Indians. They lost much of their bottom land along the river and with each successive attempt to raise the level of the dam, more Indian acres were submerged. Subsequent government settlements partially compensated the tribe for the land, but use of the land remains a point of contention.

When the American Falls project brought security to the lower valley, farmers in the upper valley agitated for increased storage facilities. As the type of agriculture changed from grain and alfalfa to row crops such as beans, sugar beets, and of course, potatoes, more water was needed. Row crops need water at a later date and need it more often. Another element that intensified the demand for more storage was the fact that the Milner, Jackson Lake, Minidoka, and American Falls dams could control the runoff, but not the source of snow and water. In other words, dry years were still frequent and were especially so throughout the depression-tainted 1930s. As prices dropped with the water level, many homesteaders were forced to give up and either sell their acres or abandon them. The farmers of the Snake River valley lost more than seven million dollars in 1935 alone.

The result of the agitation for more storage was the creation of a dam in the Snake River Canyon at beautiful Palisades, a few miles west of the Idaho-Wyoming border. Resurveyed during the 1930s, when smaller dams in the upper valley were constructed, Palisades was authorized initially in 1941, but World War II postponed construction, and the dam was again authorized in 1950. Its construction was completed in 1959, and the reservoir, which is also used extensively for recreation, was slightly smaller than American Falls. New land projects near American Falls and Rupert were opened with the increased availability of water. The effect of inflation is illustrated by the cost of the project—seventy-six million dollars—of which the farmers were to repay three-fourths by the sale of power and water shares. At the time of its completion, Palisades was the largest earth dam ever constructed by the Bureau of Reclamation. Its hydroelectric capabilities heralded the increased need for pumping and sprinkling.

By 1960, dams on the upper Snake River system stored nearly 4.5 million acre feet of water. After sixty years, a raging, wild, impassable and unpredictable stream was under control. There is no way that the Astorians, the Hudson's Bay trappers, Bonneville, Frémont, or the Oregon pioneers, could they return, would even recognize the country. The curious visitor of the nineteenth century would be most amazed by the vast array of sprinkling systems that now pervade the entire valley. Shortly after World War II, dry farmers, those who previously relied completely on nature to provide water, intensified their search for water by going underground, and they succeeded in locating a number of wells. This aspect of irrigation has produced systems all the way from Ashton to Filer and beyond. Tens of thousands of acres were reclaimed in this manner; however, the more efficient sprinkler systems depend on costly electric power to pump the water through the silvery pipe.

Just as controlled cutting is an absolute for the timber industry's survival, so is water a necessity for Idaho farmers to produce and prosper. Countless dams, including the huge Dworshak Dam on the North Fork of the Clearwater, provide recreation, flood control, and electrical power as well as irrigation water. Many of the questions and problems facing contemporary Idaho revolve around its greatest resources—water and trees. The entire southern part of the state, as well as numerous central Idaho valleys, depend on a stored water capacity, and the north needs the growing stands of timber. Consolidated timber interests and irrigation co-operation mark significant milestones in the development of the state; yet, they did not provide immunity from recession and depression, as the 1920s and 1930s tragically illustrate.

7

A Chaotic Twenty Years:
Depression and New Deal

T is a fact of Idaho's economic history that the Great Depression of 1929–1939 was only the second act of a disastrous economic drama that began after World War I. During the Great War, Idaho's main contributors to economic stability, timber, minerals, and agricultural products, had experienced sharp rises in prices. New farmland was opened for use which probably should have remained uncultivated. Old mines were reopened and exploited, and, of course, timber was cut with undue haste. The lash of profits whipped speculators of all types into action. However, the speculative bubble in agriculture was pricked shortly after the troops returned from Europe.

Farming economics are illustrative of the problems faced by Idahoans during the 1920s. While much of the country was caught up in the jazz age, Prohibition, movie stars, gangsters, and Babe Ruth, Idaho's farmers fought to survive.

Corresponding to the increase of farm prices, the cost of agricultural land and farm equipment had risen sharply. Many farmers, enjoying rare prosperity, had put their profits into more land and new machinery. If the farms did not show immediate profits, the owners borrowed to buy more land and equipment. Wartime overexpansion and the accompanying postwar inflation left Idaho and the nation's farmers in a tragic situation. The cycle had caught up with the children of the soil again. More water on more land produced greater yields, and without overseas markets upon which to dump the surplus, down went the prices. For nearly twenty years, Idaho's agricultural economy was cursed by the problem of overproduction. Still, the farmers pushed for the creation of greater dams and canal systems in order to guarantee abundant crops.

Some sample statistics should illustrate the chaos and the dilemma Idahoans faced. Idaho potatoes, which have become so noted that the words *famous potatoes* are printed on the state's license plates as well as on menus throughout the nation, brought $1.51 per bushel in 1919. Three years later, potatoes were sold at approximately thirty cents a bushel. Throughout the decade, potatoes slowly rose in value until, by 1929, the price was nearly back to the 1919 level. Then came the great crash, which by 1932 had driven the price down to less than twenty-five cents per bushel. There was no way a farmer could survive against those odds. Even if he could sell land to recover some losses, the farmer would find that potato acres for which he had paid $150 per acre at the end of the war, were worth a third of that five years later. In fact, Idaho did not recover from the agricultural depression of the 1920s until World War II. It took another war to solve the production, preservation, and marketing disasters that plagued Idaho growers. The great prosperity of the bull market in stocks never trickled into Idaho, and next to Montana, Idaho had the highest rate of emigration of any western state during the "roaring twenties."

Other specific crop prices punctuate the effect of the depression throughout Idaho. Wheat, a grain grown throughout the state, sold for nearly $2.50 per bushel at the war's end. In 1922, farmers sold their harvest for only ninety cents, which meant that they would have had to grow three times as much wheat to get the same amount of gross receipts at year's end. By 1929, the price had climbed part way back to $1.30. Sugar beets present another documentation of disaster. During the war, beets sold for $22 a ton, but in 1922 they only brought $6. The market value in the fall of 1929 was $15, $7 less than a decade earlier. The story was the same in cattle, sheep, as well as in wool, corn, peas, and lettuce. There was no guarantee that any crop would bring returns on the investment. Faced by mortgage foreclosure caused by these successive devastating losses, Idaho farmers were compelled to organize for their own salvation.

Idaho's banking institutions were also hard-hit by the economic distress. Twenty-seven Idaho banks closed their doors during the early 1920s. Seven of these were nationally chartered banks, but all twenty-seven served rural areas. Some of the banks were taken over by solvent banks, but the fact that so many had collapsed added to the suffering of the depression.

The agrarian depression of the early 1920s was nationwide, and the administration of Warren G. Harding decided to solve the problem. The official response, the Emergency Tariff of 1921 and the Fordney-McCumber Bill of 1922, only aggravated the situation. Blaming Woodrow Wilson's low tariff for the difficulties, the high Harding tariffs revised rates upward on almost all goods, agricultural and industrial. The net effect of the two tariffs was to reduce American farmers' markets overseas by reducing the earnings of foreign consumers who would have used their income to buy American products. By cutting off trade between nations, the tariffs were completely ineffective in relieving American agriculture. Many Idahoans had originally supported tariffs as a means to protect their products from foreign competition, but they soon realized the cruel hoax it perpetrated upon them. Sen. William Borah opposed the tariff bills because they increased the price farmers would have to pay for life's necessities: clothing, shoes, and fuel.

Short-sighted Idaho stockmen also involved themselves in self-defeating measures. Only a decade before Henry A. Wallace was preaching and practicing "artificial scarcity," Idaho ranchers believed that the best way they could get ahead was to raise and sell more cattle or sheep. Like so many marginal farmers, stockmen felt that if they could expand the herd and the acreage, then they could meet the mortgage and feed the family. This expansion had the effect of creating a surplus which drove the price per pound downward. Idaho's cattlemen and sheepgrowers lobbied to get previously used national forest lands reopened for more summer grazing. The ghost of Theodore Roosevelt haunted them, but they fought to regain unlimited use of the acres Roosevelt had set aside. One Idaho native, T. C. Stanford, adamantly opposed the proposal to create a Sawtooth National Park in 1922 because it would "close the gates tight against hundreds of thousands of livestock." [1] Sawtooth National Park is still discussed, but the forest service and rancher associations fought it to a standstill. As individual farmers attempted to maximize sales and minimize costs, they were only thinking of next year's payment, not the welfare of the natural and physical resources of the state.

Idaho's national representatives, realizing that the welfare of their state was tied to national and international politics, tried to work for national legislation that would alleviate the crisis. Out of this concern developed the concept of parity prices. In other words, parity prices would be proportional to the price farmers had to pay for necessities. A date would be chosen when, for example, the value of a bushel of wheat would be equivalent to the value of a pair of shoes. Then if the general price index doubled, or the price of shoes doubled, the price for wheat would correspondingly rise. Such a system was designed to guarantee that a farmer could avoid the dual evils of rising costs and declining income. Obviously, administering such a program would be a bookkeeping monstrosity. The whole question of how to handle surpluses and what to do about some products not covered by parity meant that farmers were divided about the price-parity issue.

Larger farmers, especially those who felt a kinship to the new Farm Bureau Federation, advocated co-operative action to keep prices high. Co-operatives had been tried for many years by the Mormons in Idaho, but now the supporters of co-ops envisioned creating a monopoly for a product, so that they could control the time of sale and have enough clout to bargain for a desired price. Self-sacrificing co-operative experiments in Idaho lacked success. During hard times, a farmer may have to sell at a given time, where another may have the wherewithal to wait until the

1. T. C. Stanford to Addison T. Smith, Nov. 17, 1922. Quoted in Gwynn Barrett and Leonard Arrington, "The 1921 Depression: Its Impact on Idaho," *Idaho Yesterdays* 15 (Summer 1971): 15.

price is right. Consequently, by the mid 1920s the Idaho Farm Bureau members, especially after the 1924 drought, supported parity.

The net result of this continued agitation for price parity was the twice-passed and twice-vetoed McNary-Haugen Bill. This legislation proposed that parity prices be maintained by a farm board that would be instructed to dispose of agricultural surpluses on the world market, if need be at a loss. The farmers, who would benefit from the assured high domestic prices, would be charged a tax for the cost of selling the surplus. Most agricultural areas fought for the bill, but Idaho's Senator Borah vociferously opposed the measure because it still penalized the farmer. Borah saw no need to tax the farmers for the cost of disposing of the surplus. According to him, farmers were spending much more of their income on taxes than other people, and further taxation would only increase the discrepancy. Borah, who knew how many Idaho farms were being sold at mortgage auctions, exclaimed: "How many farms now ready to be sold for taxes will you save from the hammer if you continue this inequality?" [2] Borah wanted to use five hundred million dollars of federal money to support directly the struggling farmer. It was Borah's hope that tariff profits could be used to protect American farmers. But his plea did not influence Congress or Calvin Coolidge. A depression later, another administration, that of Franklin Delano Roosevelt, would respond with direct relief to farmers.

Many farmers joined the Idaho Nonpartisan League because both political parties seemed inept at handling the agrarian crisis. The league originally had had an impact in Idaho during World War I. Included in its program was provision for a state system of storage plants, warehouses, flour mills, grain elevators, and packing plants. It also lobbied for a state-owned electrical power system which would handle both production and distribution. Since farm taxes were so high, the Nonpartisan League advocated tax exemption for farm improvements and a state operated system of rural credit banks. Few state officials

2. Claudius O. Johnson, *Borah of Idaho* (Seattle: University of Washington, 1967), p. 410.

would touch that platform. Thus after flirting with the Democratic party, the league and its members evolved into the 1920s version of the Progressive party. In the early twenties, the Progressives actually supplanted the Democrats as a major party in the state.

Nationally and within Idaho, there was no real program to alleviate the agrarian, economic, and political discontent of the early 1920s. Effective farm measures were almost impossible to develop, let alone pass. Most of the nation was involved in building homes, buying automobiles, and speculating on all industries. Herbert Hoover, an Iowan by birth and Californian by residence, seemed sympathetic to the expressed grievances of farmers. Although unwilling to co-operate with Borah's wish for a parity supported by surplus tariff dollars, Hoover did approve the creation of a Federal Farm Board. The board, which never received a fair test, encouraged co-operative marketing, but failed to handle the tricky parity problem. After the great crash of October 1929, the entire nation, not just the farmers, was caught in a downward economic spiral. The agricultural depression of the 1920s developed into the general economic disaster that engulfed all of Idaho and the rest of the states.

No longer could Idaho's farmers be only concerned about agricultural markets. The entire issue of national recovery was tied to farm, industrial, and commercial well-being. It is an erroneous assumption that farmers in agricultural states suffered least during the Great Depression. Degree of distress is difficult to quantify. Although farmers were employed and had food, they definitely were in a state of depression, and agricultural centers were devastated. Idaho ranked seventh among the states that experienced the greatest income drop. From 1929 to 1932, the average income of Idahoans was slashed by 49.3 percent. For an individual to have his income during a four-year period cut in half is a personal economic disaster. That was the fate suffered by Idahoans. In comparison, Massachusetts underwent a 30.3 percent cut, which was also tragic, yet was relatively much better than Idaho's.

If the depression of the early 1920s cut profits, the Great Depression obliterated them. By the fall of 1932, Idaho wheat sold for twenty-six cents a bushel. Cattle were often sold for less than $25 per head, and sheep brought between $2 and $3. These were the worst prices of the century. Thirty years of gains were wiped out in a few short months. Other products were similarly effected. Sugar beets dropped to an average of $4 per ton in 1932. Their value had been cut to one-fourth by the depression and the same was true of wool, which fell from thirty-six to nine cents a pound. There was simply no way for a farmer to survive, let alone prosper, in such a market. Idaho's farmers had a cash income of $116 million in 1929, but by 1932 it had fallen to slightly less than $41 million.

The timber and mineral industries were hit almost as hard as agriculture. Since there was no great demand to build, the lumber mills and retail yards closed their gates. During the Hoover administration, white pine production decreased from 438 million board feet to 169 million board feet. The unemployment of lumberjacks was matched by that among miners. Mineral production in Idaho fell from $32 million to less than $10 million during those same four years. As in agriculture, these 1933 figures were the lowest in the century. The price of Coeur d'Alene silver bottomed out at twenty-four cents an ounce. Before the crash it brought $1.39 per ounce. Ironically, as long as the United States remained on the gold standard, gold miners prospered, and the output of gold from 1929 until 1934 tripled. However, in the total economic picture, the increased demand for gold was totally inadequate to make up for the loss of silver, lead, and zinc.

Another array of statistics further illustrates the desperate plight of Idaho's economy in the depths of the depression. Farm income statistics indicate a loss of nearly two-thirds between 1929 and 1932. Wages and salaries suffered a similar fate and fell from a 1929 level of $139 million to $81 million in 1932. In real terms, this meant Idahoans experienced a drop in per capita income from $529 to $268 from 1929 until 1932. That statistical indicator was nearly halved in four short years. At the same time, more than half of the workers employed by manufacturers were laid off. When it is considered that the state's manufacturing payroll slipped from $22.5 million to slightly more than

$7 million, it is no wonder that communal and individual despair was prevalent.

National and local politicians seemed helpless in this milieu of disaster. Hoover's orthodox approach to direct relief, which was to let the states, local governments, and charity handle it, was totally unsuccessful. An attempt to salvage banking and corporate enterprises with the Reconstruction Finance Corporation was of limited value to Idaho because of the relatively small industrial investment. Farmers received minute relief when the Federal Land Bank received additional capital and the Commodity Credit Corporation and Grain Stabilization Acts were passed. These measures proved more useful to agribusinesses and wholesalers than to the small farmers, but they helped somewhat. At the state level, Gov. H. C. Baldridge and the legislature floundered on the twin rocks of indecision and ignorance.

As foreclosures increased and sheriff's auctions were held, the public mood grew desperate. A variety of economic crises and tragedies occurred. Runs on the banks hit many areas of Idaho, and numerous banking institutions failed. Lynn Driscoll, of Boise, and the head of the First Security Bank of Idaho, was courageously determined to keep the doors of that large chain open. There were three banks in Boise in 1932, and by August only First Security was operating. Anticipating a run on his bank, Driscoll had a sign painter provide a large sign that was hung over the bank's front door. The sign read: "For the Benefit of Our Patrons This Bank Will be Open Until Late Tonight. If You Want Your Money, Come and Get It!" [3] For the next few days it was nip and tuck at the Boise bank. Driscoll had a half million dollars flown in from the sister bank in Salt Lake City, but it was never used. Many large depositors simply put their money back in the bank the day after they withdrew it because their confidence returned.

It was not an uncommon occurrence for friends of a foreclosed farmer to attend the creditor auction and agree not to bid against each other. They would then purchase the horses, cattle,

3. Glen Barrett, *J. Lynn Driscoll, Western Banker* (Boise: Syms-York Co., 1974), p. 186.

and machinery for ridiculously low prices, pay the bid, and return the purchased items to the downcast farmer.

Most ominous was a series of forest fires that swept through the mountains of central Idaho during the summer of 1931. Arsonists systematically ignited the fires and then sought employment as firefighters. The epidemic of fires was so rampant that Gov. C. Ben Ross declared the counties to be in a state of insurrection, proclaimed martial law, and used the National Guard to prohibit public access to the forest lands.

As the dark days of depression continued, the political process offered few alternatives. American elections usually come by the calendar and not the crisis, so Hoover and the voters waited as the depression months became depression years. For Idaho, the alternative was flamboyant C. Ben Ross; for the nation, it was Franklin Delano Roosevelt.

Charles Benjamin Ross, the mayor of Pocatello during the 1920s, capitalized on personal popularity and Republican lethargy to win the governorship in 1930. Because the first shock waves of the Great Depression were only beginning to reach Idaho, the 1930 election was not a repudiation of the GOP; in fact, Ross was the only real Democratic winner. Republicans controlled the legislature, and both U.S. senators were members of the Republican party. Ross, an entertaining and charismatic governor, was able to push a domestic reform program through the legislature. His three most impressive achievements were the passage of a new direct primary law, a controversial state income tax, and a tax on the private power combine. So far as Idaho was concerned, the passage of tax reform was timely because, as the depression intensified, previous revenue sources were dissipated.

Idaho overwhelmingly supported Roosevelt in 1932 and reelected Ross by an even greater margin. With coattails so long, a Democratic legislature and a new Democratic senator, James D. Pope, and two congressmen were also elected. After more than a decade of continuous economic trauma, Idahoans hoped that Roosevelt's New Deal would relieve their plight. By the winter of 1932–1933, unemployment was in excess of twenty thousand, and over one thousand mortgage foreclosures had occurred during the two previous years. Delinquent taxes had risen from slightly in excess of $11,000 to the relatively astronomical figure of $400,000, and the resources in banks had declined by more than $39 million since 1930.

Many Idahoans worked for close co-operation with Roosevelt and the New Deal. State Democratic Chairman T. A. Walters served as Harold Ickes's assistant secretary of the interior, and Senator Pope was a devoted and reliable New Dealer. Gov. Ben Ross was an exception. The governor had no intellectual or philosophical commitment to the New Deal nor did he owe his position to Roosevelt. In his relationship to the federal government and the multitude of programs developed, Ross was simply a political opportunist. Any plan that seemed beneficial to Idaho he would enthusiastically support; but if a program offered nothing to Idaho or seemed inefficient, Ross would lead the critics.

During the first year of Roosevelt's administration, Ross was not supportive of the New Deal in general. The Idaho governor, on the occasion of his first meeting with the new president, proposed a $20-billion plan of public works that would employ six million workers immediately. Roosevelt's people totally ignored the "Ross Plan" and proceeded on their varied course. Ross also clashed with Roosevelt over the repeal of Prohibition but finally yielded to national and local pressure to ratify the Twenty-first Amendment. Antagonism reached such a point that by July 4, 1933, Ross was publicly lashing out against Roosevelt's "one-man rule" and many New Deal programs. Roosevelt's Idaho supporters were dismayed by their governor's actions; they fretted over the loss of money and patronage because of Ross's eccentric behavior. On the other hand, when the federal government seemed slow in distributing appropriated funds, Idaho's governor was the first to lodge a protest about bureaucratic inefficiency. In many cases, delay was caused by the lack of proper preparation on the part of the state.

Considering the deep distrust and apprehension expressed, it is amazing that Idaho received much New Deal assistance at all. Fortunately for the state, Roosevelt was not vindictive in appropriations. The Hoover programs had illustrated that the states could not regroup and recover by themselves. It was obvious that Idaho could not go it alone. In fact, so little tax revenue was generated during 1932 and 1933 that state appropriations were reduced 42 percent, and the state could barely meet its obligations. Governor Ross eventually mellowed, and Idaho not only benefitted from New Deal measures but prospered relatively.

According to per capita statistics compiled by the federal government in 1939, only seven states received more money than Idaho did from the antidepression New Deal agencies. As might be expected in a rural state, Idaho received more needed Rural Electrification Administration funds than any other. More than two million REA dollars were spent in Idaho on electric power expansion into rural communities and isolated farms. Other agriculture programs were also of great significance to Idaho. The highly controversial and ultimately unconstitutional Agriculture Adjustment Act attempted to control production and offer subsidies to individual farmers. This federal control over grassroots-level farming was despised by many, but the AAA negotiated more than seventy-three thousand production contracts in Idaho and the prices responded favorably. The cash value of Idaho crops nearly doubled between 1932 and 1936. More than $27 million were spent in Idaho by AAA.

Much more important than the REA loans and the AAA subsidies was the Farm Credit Administration. Designed as a supplement to the AAA, this agency stopped farm mortgage foreclosures by refinancing the loans through the federal land banks. Governor Ross had declared a temporary foreclosure moratorium in 1933 and the FCA provided the necessary funds to the troubled state's farmers. In all, $76 million was lent to approximately twenty thousand separate farmers. When other programs such as the Farm Security Administration, the Commodity Credit Corporation, and federally funded research grants are added to the above programs, the end product was over $120 million spent in Idaho on agriculture. The agricultural New Deal not only assisted many Idaho farmers in their attempt to weather the depression storm but also simultaneously put money in their hands that could be spent on consumer items.

Perhaps the most popular New Deal agency was the Civilian Conservation Corps, and the CCC had a definite and exciting impact in Idaho. On the per capita basis, the $57 million spent in Idaho ranks second in CCC expenditures. For the state with millions of acres in national forests and millions more in the Bureau of Land Management, CCC projects were made to order. Eventually 18,200 young men came to Idaho and worked in the seventy mountain fresh-air camps. Building fences, roads, trails, bridges, and campgrounds, the corpsmen prepared much forest land for public use. They also treated millions of infected trees for rust fungus, worked on reforestation, and developed projects to curtail erosion. As was true in most areas, the CCC was administered smoothly in Idaho, and there was considerable local support. The beautiful scenery and clean air enticed many corpsmen to remain in the state upon completion of their tour. As one former CCC employee described it to a U.S. forest ranger, "I was infected by a contagious bug called Idaho mountain fever and it was just too pleasant to leave." [4]

Idaho profited from numerous other agencies as well. The short-lived Civil Works Administration operated only during the winter of 1933–1934, but spent about $5.5 million in Idaho, which placed the Gem State in second position among all the states where CWA funds were expended. The state ranked fourth in public works grants, sixth in public roads subsidies, and ninth in Federal Emergency Relief. To be fully understood, these statistics and vast sums of money must be translated into human welfare. For example the $20 million lent or insured by the Home Owners Loan Corporation and Federal Housing Authority meant that more than 15 percent of all nonfarm homes in the state were either saved from foreclosure or constructed by federal funds. In total, more than $331 million was spent or lent in Idaho between 1933 and 1939, and although the state remained solvent, spending did not guarantee the Democratic party political supremacy nor could vast sums of money control nature.

One of the most severe droughts of Idaho history cursed the

4. Interview by author with James L. Bruce, Dec. 19, 1966, Montpelier, Idaho. Mr. Bruce was a forest ranger throughout the entire New Deal period and was involved with various CCC operations.

state in 1934. With available water at slightly more than 50 percent of normal, crop losses were estimated at $22.4 million. Lacking adequate water, the half-filled Snake River dams provided some relief, but the Idaho dust bowl was so devastating that thirty thousand people in the irrigation districts needed direct assistance. Statistically, it was the driest year on record, and Governor Ross did not hesitate to seek federal aid. The veteran governor reported:

> Thousands of springs that have been used for watering livestock in the mountains have become dry and water must be furnished from other sections. . . . With assistance of the Federal Government we will be able to sustain our people in their homes without evacuation.[5]

If Idahoans were able to keep their homes in 1934, thousands of families in the southern Great Plains were not so lucky. Although Idaho's economy remained distressed throughout the thirties, there was a net in-migration during the decade. Many of the destitute farmers from Kansas, Oklahoma, and Texas made their way into Idaho. This influx added to the overburdened relief load, but other New Deal programs were devised to assist in a sustained recovery.

During 1935, it seemed that Idaho's state officials had to work full time trying to keep track of New Deal measures and agencies. Some programs required state participation, while others were administered solely by the federal government. The New Deal was adding genuine reform to its other goals of direct relief and recovery. Two of the most important pieces of second New Deal legislation were the Social Security Act and the National Labor Relations Act. Idaho did well in establishing state matching social security funds to take care of the blind, disabled, and dependent children. Although hard pressed, Governor Ross was able to move the state into active participation in the program. Because of the small labor population in Idaho, the NLRA did not dramatically affect unions within Idaho. However, two incidents of labor unrest during the unsettled

5. Leonard J. Arrington, "Idaho and the Great Depression," *Idaho Yesterdays* 13 (Summer 1969): 2–8.

years of 1935 and 1936 illustrate the hazard of holding office during times of crisis. In the fall of 1935, migrant farm workers in the Teton Valley struck against the pea growers because of low wages and deplorable living conditions. Ross hastily declared martial law and sent the Idaho National Guard to maintain order. There was no violence and the migrants' grievances were legitimate and acute; so Ross was condemned by liberals for acting too hastily. The next year the Industrial Workers of the World tried to organize lumberjacks in the Clearwater area of northern Idaho. The resulting dispute led to an interchange of gunfire, and, although there was no bloodshed, the strike precipitated the call for state troops again. In this instance Ross was applauded for being a good law and order man.

For depression-struck Idaho perhaps the most significant act passed in 1935 was the one that created the Works Progress Administration, headed by Harry Hopkins. The WPA offered relief and reform in a variety of ways. Hopkins, who allegedly made the statement: "We will spend and spend and elect and elect," ultimately authorized more than $22 million for Idaho projects, which consisted of 510 different buildings, roads, dams, canals, and numerous other programs. The WPA's impact on individuals in Idaho is illustrated by the following example: For one young farmer with a small family, a WPA road project provided a steady job, which was sorely needed to supplement the farm income. He hired himself and his team of horses for $4 per day during the summers of 1935 and 1936. This cash income of $100 a month was a lifesaver. This case was representative of many throughout the state.

One of the unique features of the WPA was the hiring of unemployed professionals such as teachers, actors, and musicians. Out of this thinking came the effort to produce a guidebook for every state and Washington, D. C. Idaho's effort in producing this book under the auspices of the Federal Writers' Project was a unique and frustrating, yet exciting, endeavor.

Harry Hopkins was influenced to include a writers' project in the WPA shortly after the legislation was authorized. Idaho was most fortunate that Vardis Fisher, a brilliant novelist, was chosen to direct the Gem State's endeavor. Fisher was an Idaho-born University of Chicago Ph.D. who had taught advanced composition and English literature at three universities. By the mid-1930s, Fisher had returned to his father's farm near Ririe and was writing fulltime. Although a number of his novels were published, the family income was precarious, and he accepted the $2,300 per year writers' project director's salary and moved to Boise. After initial bureaucratic problems with the state WPA were resolved, Fisher settled into the task of hiring competent assistants. Since many national leaders, WPA administrators, and Idaho citizens questioned the writers' project experiment, it was not easy for Vardis Fisher to find able assistants. Ezra Pound, the Idaho-born poet, was in Europe and Ernest Hemingway, who later moved to Ketchum, had not yet discovered the splendor of Idaho. Finally, the crusty and independent Fisher concluded that he would have to write most of the material himself and hired stenographers, typists, and secondary source researchers.

Eventually, Fisher received some aid from the state university in Moscow, its branch in Pocatello, and the Forest Service, but the project experienced a rapid turnover in personnel. Since writers' project wages were so low, as soon as Fisher trained an individual, he or she usually found a better-paying state or federal job. Still, Vardis Fisher produced a manuscript at a rapid rate. The Idaho director set a goal to complete the nation's first WPA guidebook. In addition to bureaucratic regulations and the lack of unified instructions, the frustrations inflicted upon Fisher and his associates by the Washington-based censors and editors were extreme. The censors watched for pro-Communist statements and deleted also passages concerning intragovernmental controversies as well as references to such subjects as the contentions between railroads and truckers. What nearly drove Fisher to complete distraction, however, was the occasion when editors in Washington took it upon themselves to tell him that the Grand Teton National Park was located in Idaho and that an existing natural bridge near Arco did not exist—because they had never heard of it.

Fisher negotiated a contract with the Caxton Printers of Caldwell, and publication date was set for January 1937. When the assistant national director, Henry Alsberg, received word of this fact, he initiated numerous stall tactics. Demands for revision, rewriting, and massive textual and organizational changes poured out of the national office. Near the point of total exasperation, Fisher finally discovered the real reason for delay. According to Alsberg, if the Idaho guide were to be published first, it would be an embarrassment to the total project. They wanted the guidebook for the nation's capital to be first, then those of some of the larger states before they published the book for a smaller, less-important state like Idaho. Fisher bluntly replied that the volume was completed, and it would be published, whether appropriate or not. Consistently refusing to make other suggested alterations, Fisher worked with Caxton, and the guide was published as scheduled in January 1937. It was the first completed in the nation and received excellent professional and journalistic reviews. Soon Alsberg was shipping the *Idaho Guide* to other state directors with the instruction that "this is how to do it." The Idaho novelist's own assessment of the project is interesting, but very typical: "Government is waste, but if we can get a certain percentage of our tax money back in productive things or things which add not only to the economic but to the cultural life of the nation we should be glad for it." [6] By the time the Idaho writers' project ended in 1940, the *Idaho Encyclopedia, Idaho Lore,* and several smaller publications were successfully completed. Fisher was able to move to a beautiful spot in the Hagerman Valley and produce quality novels for another three decades.

Although the writers' project enjoyed tremendous success in Idaho, Harry Hopkins, who administered all WPA projects, found it difficult to work well with Gov. C. Ben Ross. All together nearly $23 million was spent on WPA projects in the state, but Ross and Hopkins clashed over another agency, the Federal Emergency Relief Administration. Ross liked programs such as the CWA and WPA, which funneled federal funds into the state, but the FERA demanded that the state produce some matching funds. Essentially, these federal monies were appro-

6. Ronald W. Taber, "Vardis Fisher and the 'Idaho Guide': Preserving Culture for the New Deal," *Pacific Northwest Quarterly* 59 (April 1968): 68–76.

priated for direct relief, and since Idaho was evading partial financing, Idaho's was a federally financed, state administered relief program. Hopkins finally decided that unless Ross could provide some state revenue, the federal relief checks would be terminated. This ultimatum put Ross in a difficult bind, because he was committed to lowering the property tax. His only alternative appeared to be a hated 2 percent regressive sales tax. As the legislature debated and discussed, Ross grew impatient and perplexed. Finally, Ross forced the legislature's hand by closing every relief office until the sales tax was passed. Ross's coercive measures only provided a temporary victory because a statewide referendum defeated the tax the next year, 1936.

Ross, although an opportunist, had a good point in criticizing the constantly changing New Deal relief program. He agreed that unemployment relief was a federal responsibility and the works projects were preferable to a permanent direct relief alternative. However, Ross definitely disliked the confusing and conflicting number of New Deal agencies. While Roosevelt was attempting to prime the pump at all levels, Ross was caught in the middle, and the relief controversy not only highlighted his difficulties, but contributed to his demise as an Idaho politician.

By 1936 there was no doubt that Idaho had climbed part way out of the depression. Democratic politicians could point to the fact that farm income had risen 20 percent, silver and gold production was way up, and the increase in the timber harvest was substantial. With agriculture, minerals, and lumber on their way back, Roosevelt's administration was popular in Idaho. Governor Ross believed that he deserved much of the credit for the state of affairs, and in spite of his problems with Hopkins and relief, he decided that if there were ever a time to beat William Borah, it would be now. Ross failed to realize that his independent course and constant bickering with the national party leadership had alienated many Idaho Democrats. According to one source, the anti-Ross Democrats promised Roosevelt's re-election organization that if Roosevelt would endorse Borah, the Democrats would guarantee Borah's support for New Deal programs. Since Borah was then campaigning for the Republican party presidential nomination to oppose Roosevelt, this ridiculous proposal was dismissed by both the president and the senator.

The gods that guided Ben Ross erred in 1936. William Borah trounced the three-term governor by more than fifty thousand votes. Since the other Democrats in the state won easily, Borah's victory was a great personal achievement. However, 1936 was the year of the last gasp of New Deal politics in Idaho. The Democratic party remained badly split after the election, and conservatives plotted to dismantle the machinery of the pro-Roosevelt officeholders. No single man nor group of Democrats was able to hold the coalition together. The party splits became so pronounced that even Roosevelt loyalist Sen. James Pope was defeated in a primary in 1938. The new open primary enabled several thousand Republicans to cross over and elect D. Worth Clark, a conservative congressman and an isolationist. Since Roosevelt had endorsed Pope and was involved in various purges of disloyal Democrats, the outcome in Idaho significantly and personally hurt the president.

As a lasting political revolution, the New Deal failed in Idaho. The Democrats demonstrated the ability for infighting and squabbling. The governors, Ross and his successor, Barzilla Clark, were never full and complete supporters of Roosevelt. Ultimately the Idaho New Deal died as it was born, in a scuffle of factions. Its political legacy was a badly divided and basically ineffective Democratic party. Roosevelt would have preferred to prolong and develop a new approach to federal-state problems and relations, but most states, like Idaho, were not ready for such a broad and sweeping reform.

Roosevelt and his national party leader, James Farley, never attacked Ross and his supporters. Instead, they tried to work with both the Pope faction and the Ross faction, and the final result was a disrupted and fragmented organization. Consequently, the New Deal did not radically alter internal politics within Idaho. There was a brief period when liberal Democrats gained supremacy, but it was an interlude, and the state remained fairly conservative.

As war came, the state's impulse for change, like that of the federal government, was overshadowed by international concerns. There were no long-term Idaho state-sponsored reforms that achieved great success. Idaho's attempts to modernize decent welfare and public health programs bogged down and died. The depression-born sales tax, which might have paid the fare for social welfare projects, lasted only two years and was not resurrected for three decades.

On the other hand, however, the total impact of the Roosevelt response to the Great Depression was keenly felt and appreciated in Idaho. In retrospect, it seems that the New Deal was not a vast barbecue to which any and all could come and lunch at the public trough. One of the comparative realities of the Roosevelt program was that so little was spent. The entire national endeavor cost approximately $24 billion, about half as much as the United States spent on lend-lease during World War II. In fact, a lesson of the war was that the recovery efforts of the 1930s were not widespread enough nor were they adequate. That is one reason the New Deal dragged through the entire decade. But in terms of balancing the human budget and propounding the philosophy that money is expendable and humanity is not, the New Deal was successful inside of Idaho. Strip away internal politics and the failure to maintain a solid Democratic coalition, and there were some amazing achievements during the 1930s within the borders of the state.

Most importantly, the agricultural depression that had dragged on for nearly two decades was finally overcome by the price supports, loans, and subsidies of the New Deal. Tens of thousands of Idaho farms were saved by the New Deal agencies. More than four thousand Idahoans were employed on an expanded highway program that not only constructed and improved thousands of miles of roads, but also brought the geographically divided state better communications. The Owyhee Reclamation Project and the Arrowrock Dam were completed and added significantly to Idaho's unique phenomena of countless canals and irrigation reservoirs. A list of WPA and PWA projects includes twenty-five airports, seventy-eight educational buildings, numerous parks, and more than one hundred public buildings, sewer systems, waterworks, athletic fields, and fairgrounds. It is probable that these projects would eventually have been completed during normal times, but the recovery mentality created a feeling of urgency and crisis. If there was a question of now or later, most opportunistic Idahoans, like their New Deal governor, Ben Ross, chose now without hesitation.

As a result of this heavy influx of federal funds, the state's economy responded. By 1939 individual income taxes had risen to $628,000 from the 1933 figure of $138,000. Corporation taxes increased six times so that by 1939 they were nearly $1.4 million. The per capita income of Idaho's citizens was $287 in 1933, but six years later it was $452. Banks, which had been threatened by the agrarian depression for years, were solvent, and individual deposits more than doubled from 1933 to 1939. By the end of the decade, $90 million was in the banks. Farming, mining, and the timber industry all experienced partial recovery by 1939, and Idaho was prepared to participate in the titantic struggle for survival throughout the world.

It took the war economy to solve ultimately the decade-long unemployment problem. Federal funds were shifted from public works to the construction of weaponry. During the war, Idaho had two major military bases and a naval ordnance plant at Pocatello. Mountain Home Air Force Base and Farragut Naval Base on Lake Pend Oreille were created. One of the infamous Japanese-American Relocation centers was in Minidoka County north of Rupert. However, Idaho's Japanese-American farmers in the Snake River valley survived the war with little persecution. For Idaho, World War II meant the end of a depression that had lasted twenty years. The 1920s, the depression, the New Deal and the war illustrated that Idaho was a genuine part of the nation and that the nation's ills had to be shared by all. They also demonstrated that as a western state, Idaho was treated very well by Roosevelt's New Deal. These decades also highlighted a unique independent political heritage that has become a feature of the state's history.

8

The Politics of Diversity

IDAHO'S politics are usually personal rather than partisan. Ideology notwithstanding, Idahoans vote for persons, not parties or labels. For example, in the 1966 primary, the GOP voters defeated their nationally prominent moderate Republican governor, Robert E. Smylie, and replaced him with an avowed ultraconservative, Donald W. Samuelson. That same year, conservative Sen. Len B. Jordan also won easily. Two years later an ultraconservative congressman, George Hansen, decided that the trend was predictable and challenged the very liberal senator, Frank Church. Church was a critic of the Vietnam War, a proponent of conservation, and a supporter of civil rights. Samuelson and Jordan had won, and Richard Nixon's coattails were available, so George Hansen jumped on for a ride to glory. Church trounced the overconfident challenger by nearly a two-to-one majority. Nixon easily defeated Humphrey in Idaho, and even George Wallace did well.

In 1962, Idaho had two Senate seats available, and Church and Jordan both won. Although Church won by a greater margin, Jordan survived, the voters thus demonstrating their ideological flexibility.

Idaho voters had expressed their pleasure with the New Deal by casting their 1936 votes for Franklin Delano Roosevelt and at the same time overwhelmingly re-electing William E. Borah, who often voted against Roosevelt and for a brief time pursued the Republican nomination in order to run against him. It is not uncommon to have Idaho's senators, representatives, and state officials split on every major national or local issue. Personalities in Idaho have always prevailed over ideologies.

Idaho's voting patterns may not be unique, actually, but they do reveal a characteristic frontier political independence. Idaho's first decade of statehood politics was marked by some phenomena every bit as significant as the disfranchisement of Mormon voters. The great western issue of free silver, which meant that the westerners wanted the United States to return to a bimetal standard in order to curb deflation, brought Idaho's farmers' alliances into collusion with the Knights of Labor. The result was the emergence of the Populist party of Idaho. By 1892, the Populists had joined with enough silver Republicans and disgruntled Democrats so that Idaho's first electoral votes were cast for the Populist, Gen. James B. Weaver. Grover Cleveland, the national winner, received only two popular votes in the entire state. National Democrats had encouraged their local counterparts to join the Populists in order to keep electoral votes from the Republicans. With this inauspicious beginning, confused by the fact that Idaho's first state legislature elected four United States senators instead of two, Idaho's political history commenced. The story of the election of four senators demonstrates the chaos caused by bad timing and political chicanery. Shortly after statehood was granted Idaho, it was discovered that in order for one-third of the total Senate seats to be available every two years, one Idaho senator would be elected for six years, another for two, and a third to serve for only a few months, or until the six-year term began. Why the legislature did not elect the same man to the four-month and the six-year term is explained as follows: The legislature chose George Shoup, Fred Dubois, and William McConnell; then the three men drew lots for the tenure of office. McConnell drew the short term, Dubois the full term, and Shoup the middle. McConnell was from northern Idaho, and since he drew the short term, that section felt cheated. At least William H. Claggett, a former crony of Dubois, felt so. Claggett persuaded the Democrats in the legislature to join north Idaho Republicans and elect Claggett to the same six-year term that had already been given to Dubois. Ultimately Claggett contested Dubois's election in the United States Senate, but he got nowhere.

With such confused beginnings it is no wonder that the first two decades of Idaho's political history were chaotic. Fred Dubois rode his two favorite crusades—anti-Mormonism and free silver—from the Republicans to the Silver Republicans and finally to the Democrats. Dubois could drag his loyal supporters from one political label to another without a great concern for more than the longevity of his political machine. This type of mentality has always been part of the state's heritage. The people are attracted to, and swayed by, a powerful individual, not a platform or a philosophy. The entire progressive movement in Idaho illustrates this reality.

Progressives belonged to both major parties and some insignificant splinter groups. For the most part, in the western states they were the believers in direct election of senators, direct primaries, the initiative, referendum, recall, and the secret ballot. Like many western states, Idaho was early in granting the vote to women. Many of these democratic reforms were heirlooms of the Populist party, but it took the progressives to achieve implementation. Some progressives might support Theodore Roosevelt's conservation program, while others wanted federal intervention in and control of any corporation involved in interstate commerce. Social abuses such as child labor, mining conditions, and slum prevention also attracted the attention of progressives. The entire movement was designed to improve the quality of life for Americans as well as to increase participatory democracy. Idaho was in the forefront of many battles that led to much-needed reforms.

In Idaho, progressives were often at odds on specific issues, and there was a constant battle over shades of progressivism. Fred Dubois fought against direct primaries and wanted to restrict democracy among the Mormons, but he supported conservation. His Senate counterpart, Weldon Heyburn, fought Roosevelt viciously on conservation and opposed the direct election of senators; yet he was Senate sponsor of the Pure Food and Drug Act. William Borah, who succeeded Dubois in the Senate, was a leader in the move to adopt a national graduated income tax amendment, and also supported appropriations for western reclamation projects. An advocate of expanded democracy, Borah sponsored the amendment which turned the Senate election process over to the people.

Idaho progressives had a problem with the full sweep of progressive reform. While most Idahoans liked reclamation, they were either lukewarm or openly hostile to the concept of federally controlled forest and mineral reserves. It was a case of wanting to have the cake and eat it as well. The prosperity that accompanied land, timber, and mineral exploitation was coveted, but the preservation and conservation phases also were attractive. The entire concept of conservation has been controversial within Idaho since Theodore Roosevelt made it a crusade of his type of progressivism. Political progressivism was much less controversial, yet necessary to the development of Idaho. The bitter dispute over a direct primary law and Prohibition replaced anti-Mormonism as the leading political issues early in the twentieth century. Both major parties split along progressive lines over what to support and what to oppose. However, the tide of progressivism surged forward, and Idaho passed a local-option liquor law as well as a provision for a direct primary in 1909.

Other progressive measures were passed in the subsequent years and reflected national trends as well as Idaho goals. Gov. James Hawley, a Democrat, was in office when state constitutional amendments, which validated the participatory concepts of the initiative, referendum, and the recall, were passed. The national progressives wanted to break the rule of political bosses, in order that direct primaries, initiatives, referendums, and recalls could achieve that goal. Idaho was one of the first states to institute these reforms. A state board of education and other technical agencies were also authorized to handle specific departments. The political appointee was to be replaced by the skilled and educated expert or technician. The city commission form of government was also approved as another advance for popular government. Before the progressive movement ended, Idaho's legislature had created a public utilities commission, a highway commission, and other agencies to protect the public and provide for the orderly development of the state. It did not matter whether the individual politician was a Republican, Democrat, or a Progressive, for the first fifteen years of the twentieth century, progressivism was the key to Idaho political success. However, the national movement, except for Prohibition, had run its course by the time America entered World War I.

Idaho's progressive destiny was left in the hands of German-born Moses Alexander, the first elected Jewish governor in the United States. His victory in 1914 created considerable notoriety for Idaho. It was a novelty to see Borah and Walter Johnson (of Weiser), the great Washington Senator baseball pitcher, replaced on the nation's front pages by another Idahoan. People were taken by the new governor's religion, but they really did not know much about him or his platform. The competent and attractive Alexander, a Democrat, had served as Boise's mayor prior to seeking the governorship.

In the progressive tradition, Governor Alexander persuaded the legislature to pass a workmen's compensation act and to create a state insurance fund. It was also during Alexander's administration that Idaho's legislature adopted a constitutional amendment that forbade the manufacture or sale of alcoholic beverages. In fact, Idaho went dry before the nation's Eighteenth Amendment was even proposed. Consequently, the era of bootleggers and moonshiners lasted two decades in Idaho, from 1916 to 1935. The national issues of enforcement and expense, as well as the question of whether or not it was possible to create a genuinely dry paradise, were faced early in Idaho, and ultimately the moral crusades of both state and nation were found wanting. In 1935, during C. Ben Ross's last term as governor, a system of state-owned liquor stores was developed to control the revenue and the sale of hard liquor. Bootlegging ceased and the much-needed revenue flowed into the state treasury.

Alexander failed to win legislative approval for a complete overhaul of the state government, in part because of increased interest in World War I and a new criminal syndicalism act.

This act was directed against the Industrial Workers of the World, who were trying to organize the loggers of northern Idaho. The act, clearly a wartime measure, declared that any advocacy of armed revolution was a criminal offense. Although Alexander professed sympathy toward the labor movement and preferred other devices for dealing with antiwar radicals, he signed the act and hoped it would control Big Bill Haywood and the IWW. In effect, however, it was such legislation, added to the federal Alien, Sedition, and Espionage Acts, that led to a wholesale violation of civil liberties.

Lashed into a patriotic frenzy by the great crusade to make the world safe for democracy, many Idahoans became extremists in their efforts to provide prowar unanimity. A state council of defense was organized, and its influence spread to the county and community level. Criticism of the war effort was not condoned, and any German-American was automatically suspected of subversion or disloyalty. Governor Alexander, who was a native of Germany, was a sane administrator during the frenzy caused by the patriotic councils of defense. He resisted demands for around-the-clock troop protection of reservoirs, railroad centers, and electrical power plants. Alexander's hesitancy caused many state leaders to call for the creation of "home guards" to protect vital properties from potential sabotage. Other individuals accused the Bavarian-born Alexander of overt disloyalty, and one individual demanded an investigation to determine how much Kaiser Wilhelm influenced the Idaho governor.

Alexander's policies were tested during a logger's strike in the summer of 1917. Although there were some IWW organizers and workers involved, most millowners and the press felt that the whole strike was German-planned and fomented. Industry and the councils of defense insisted on martial law in northern Idaho, but Governor Alexander resisted the pressure and refused to call out the troops. Instead, he utilized the criminal syndicalism law and urged county sheriffs in northern Idaho to arrest any strikers who had preached or resorted to violence. Alexander then toured the strike area and encouraged the loggers and sawmill workers to return to their jobs. In effect, the

"Wobblies" were driven from the state, and industrial peace returned to the Panhandle by the fall of 1917.

The growing fear of labor disorder and German espionage continued as home guards drilled and patriotic leagues and protective associations formed. The degree of patriotism of German-Americans was always an issue, and any disloyal act or statement was quickly seized upon as ammunition for the extreme patriots. An owner of a facsimile gold-plated iron cross was jailed in Pocatello, and an angry mob of teachers in Lincoln County threw one of their colleagues into the Wood River because his behavior had been "traitorous." When snoopy citizens discovered a photograph of Wilhelm in a Troy hotel room, they roughed up the owner, and after having destroyed the picture, the mob forced the man to "kiss the Stars and Stripes." In eastern Idaho a group of enforcers disguised their identity in the masks and robes of the Ku Klux Klan and went out to find pro-Germans. German-dominated churches, such as the Dunkards, were constantly harassed during the war, and their pastors were subjected to continual surveillance.

Idaho's wartime experience with vigilantes and radicals was similar to that of many other states and the entire nation. Civil liberties were abused because of the national origin of many citizens, and there was a noticeable inability on the part of Idaho's self-styled patriots to distinguish between peaceful radicals or genuine revolutionaries. Although free speech suffered at the hands of the wartime vigilantes, Idahoans did not resort to capital punishment or extreme violence. The same can be said of the "Red Scare" which followed the war-ending international armistice by only a few months.

In reality, the national Red Scare of 1919–1920 never affected Idaho very much. The Idaho version of the Red Scare dovetailed with the vicious anti-German hysteria of the war and was directed against Socialists and a new organization, the Idaho Nonpartisan League, rather than hard-core or suspected Bolsheviks. The Red Scare in Idaho was geared to local issues and not international conspiracies. Socialists had consistently opposed the American involvement in World War I, and many national leaders such as Kate Richards O'Hare, James Maurer, and Emil Siedel came to Idaho to agitate against the war. The Socialist party was especially adamant about encouraging draft resistance, and since Governor Alexander had refused to dismiss a Socialist draft board member in Rupert, the patriotic groups resorted to city statutes that controlled all meetings and consequently avoided confrontation with the fair-minded governor. It is significant that William Borah stood firmly against these wartime excesses and supported amnesty for all political prisoners after the war.

In mid-1917, a new force moved into Idaho that greatly upset the defenders against radicalism. The Idaho Nonpartisan League was organized by newcomers associated with a similar group in North Dakota. The INPL advocated a type of agrarian socialism that included state-owned elevators, warehouses, processing plants, electric power systems, and credit-banks. Ideologically similar to the Populists, the Nonpartisan League blasted corporate evils, especially the power trust, food processors, and corporations that profited from the war. Farmer's Union and Grange officials heartily endorsed the radical platform by 1918, and some conservative Idahoans quickly associated the INPL with the "Wobblies" and Socialists.

Although many politicians, newspapers, and the councils of defense described the INPL as "Northwest Bolsheviki" and "State Communists," the militant farmers supported the war effort by buying bonds and supporting the Red Cross. However, a few fearful citizens believed the class conflict prognosticated by the Socialists was at hand. The Socialists did try to support the INPL in its efforts to organize Idaho farmers, but failed to control the political behavior of the league. In fact, in 1918, the INPL slated their candidates on the Democratic party ticket, which led to a split party and ensured Republican victories. Republicans campaigned against the Nonpartisan League with such slogans as "The fight is on against the plan of a non-partisan league to set up a Bolshevistic government in Idaho." To further illustrate the gymnastic character of Idaho politics, it is interesting to note that the INPL supported William E. Borah, a Republican, for re-election.

Idaho's politics during World War I and immediately after were marred by repressive measures curtailing the activities of dissenters and radicals. The Red Scare danger was not so pronounced in Idaho, and consequently the suppression was much lighter than in other areas of the nation. For the most part, the radicalism of Socialists, IWW's, and Nonpartisans was handled at the ballot box, not at bridge trestles or at lynching trees. Fear tactics and ignorance were common, but the state emerged with few scars on the body politic. It was left for a number of individualistic politicians to guide the state toward the present.

It is dangerous to single out only a few of the numerous politicians who have served Idaho. Many individuals have contributed significantly to the state's political development. In order to pursue the theme of the personal nature of Idaho's politics, however, it is necessary to discuss a select number of elected officials whose careers exemplify that quality. It seems that many of Idaho's congressmen of both parties and districts have only used their office to try to attain a seat in the Senate and have lacked the patience to remain in the House of Representatives and make a career there. A few, D. Worth Clark, Henry Dworshak, and James McClure, have succeeded in that oft-used tactic, while others, Compton White, Gracie Pfost, and George Hansen, failed. Only a pair of congressmen, Burton French, who served thirteen terms in the House during the Borah years, and his counterpart, Addison Smith, who was elected ten times, seemed content in their role. And of those two, Smith constantly flirted with the potential of a higher call. Gracie Pfost, a very able congresswoman in the 1950s and early 1960s, had the potential to be a power in the House, but she submitted to the siren call and went after a Senate seat.

Another interesting feature is that a majority of defeated Idaho senators left the state to try to build a career elsewhere. Fred T. Dubois and John Nugent obtained federal appointments, as did James Pope, who was appointed by Roosevelt to be a director of the Tennessee Valley Authority. Following his stint with TVA, the former Boise mayor remained in Knoxville and established a law firm. Glen Taylor, a persistent candidate, lived in California between the elections of 1940, 1942, and

1944. The former country-western singer would return to the
state for a campaign. When he was defeated in the first two general elections, Taylor packed up his family and returned to the
defense plants of California. Taylor finally won in 1944, but
was defeated in a 1950 primary. Back to California he went.
His comeback attempt thwarted in 1954 and 1956, Taylor left
Idaho and moved to California where he manufactured the Taylor Topper, an exclusive toupee. Herman Welker and D. Worth
Clark followed the course of many struck with "Potomac
Fever." They remained in Washington, D.C., after their defeats
and worked as lawyers and lobbyists.

One of the most significant elements in the political history of
Idaho has been the use and misuse of the direct primary election. The open primary enables members of one party to cross
over and vote in the other party's primary against a candidate
they desire defeated. Such a system encourages party switching
in order to defeat strong opposition candidates in a primary. A
few blatant examples involve the Democratic party from 1938 to
1950. In 1938, conservative Congressman D. Worth Clark
edged liberal incumbent James Pope in a surprising victory in
the senatorial primary. Thousands of Republicans voted in the
Democratic primary because they felt Clark would be easier to
defeat in the general election. Although Clark won, the same
philosophy existed six years later when Glen Taylor, a liberal
maverick, upset Clark by less than two hundred votes in the
primary and went on to a general election victory. Clark returned the favor six years later after Taylor left the Democratic
party and became the vice-presidential candidate on Henry A.
Wallace's Progressive party ticket. During the hectic days of the
cold war, Taylor's criticism of the American containment
foreign policy left him totally vulnerable. Clark defeated Taylor
by less than a thousand votes in the primary, but was defeated
by the red-baiting Herman Welker in the general election.

The Smylie-Samuelson story is also a vivid example of the
strange vicissitudes of Idaho's primary politics. Robert Smylie,
an experienced lawyer and the state's attorney general for one
term, was elected governor three times and decided to seek a
fourth term in 1966. A governor who served longer than any

other person in Idaho history, the Iowa-born Smylie had shown a steady, but unspectacular administrative capability for the first ten years of his tenure. In the last two years of his administration, Smylie moved into the national limelight as a leader of the Republican governors' conference and as the first prominent Republican to call for a reorganization of the party after Barry Goldwater's 1964 debacle. It was also in his final two years that he pushed through a number of controversial progressive reforms. Most important was the passage of the sales tax, which revamped the entire tax structure and let the state assume a large share of local school taxes. Smylie also was able to get a state park and recreation program approved, which included persuading the Harriman family to will its beautiful "Railroad Ranch" near Yellowstone National Park to the state. However, ultraconservative Republicans, upset over Smylie's treatment of Goldwater, ambushed Smylie in the 1966 primary by running Don Samuelson, who, as a state senator, had opposed nearly every one of Smylie's proposals. It is no wonder that Idaho's historical graveyard primaries prompt contemporary politicians to avoid overconfidence as they contemplate their political future. A convention-primary system was tried in an attempt to avoid these potential evils, but still proved unworkable because of the undemocratic nature of conventions.

Smylie knew that the ultraconservative, right wing of his party had to be reckoned with, but he underestimated their power. Since World War II, Idaho has elected a number of politicians whose appeal was directed toward preventing internal subversion and external communist expansion. Herman Welker supported Joseph McCarthy to the very end and used McCarthy-type tactics in the 1950 and 1954 elections within Idaho. It is difficult to gauge whether or not Welker was sincere in his support for McCarthy, but his better legacy to the state was in obtaining professional baseball contracts for two western Idaho standouts, Vernon Law, of Meridian, with the Pittsburgh Pirates, and Harmon Killebrew, of Payette, with the old Washington Senators. Congressmen Steve Symms and George Hansen encouraged right-wing support and their campaign strategies occasionally utilized the technique of the "soft on Communism" charge, especially when they were attacking Frank Church. As a governor, Don Samuelson fit this pattern as well.

Yet, in spite of this post World War II conservatism, which is apparent in many rural and agricultural states, Idaho maintained a progressive tradition. It is still the personalities that determine the outcome of Idaho's elections. Fred Dubois, C. Ben Ross, Glen Taylor, and James Pope were basically liberal in policies and philosophies, but the two men who have carried the progressive banner the farthest in the twentieth century are Senators William E. Borah and Frank Church. Together, they have been elected ten times and have served over fifty years. In fact, Church technically occupies Borah's former Senate seat. In foreign policy, domestic reform, and national recognition, Borah and Church are in a class of their own. Their collective stories are illustrative of the development of Idaho and the nation during the twentieth century.

Born in Illinois the year the Civil War ended, William E. Borah came to Idaho in 1890, Idaho's statehood year. For half a century, this dedicated and eloquent man was intimately involved with the state and the nation. Borah's legal abilities were ably demonstrated by his honesty, fairness, and brilliance in the cases involving Diamondfield Jack, the Coeur d'Alene miners, and Big Bill Haywood. He married the daughter of William J. McConnell, an Idaho governor, and quickly moved into Republican political circles. Borah is best known for his foreign policy involvement during and immediately after World War I. Described by opponents as an ardent and egotistical isolationist, the Idaho senator is accused of subverting Woodrow Wilson's plan for international peace by blocking the League of Nations. Borah was in the national political limelight for nearly thirty-four years, and his career has been criticized, scrutinized, and dissected for the three and one-half decades since his death. An objective assessment concludes that William E. Borah was very much in the tradition of Idaho personal politics, and, in part, explains why he was sent to Washington for six successive terms and why partisan accusations that national and international affairs forced him to forget Idaho are unfounded.

As an attorney in Boise, Borah realized early that the real future of Idaho was in the soil, the forests, and the water. He worked consistently for reclamation projects that would benefit Idaho, and he pressured the Taft, Harding, and Coolidge administrations for a variety of federally supported projects. Borah also fought against Canadian reciprocity agreements desired by President Taft because he believed farmers would suffer from the competition. As a freshman senator, Borah was responsible for obtaining a liberal revision of the Homestead Law so that three-years' occupancy of the land was all that was needed prior to patenting, and through his efforts some marginal timber lands were opened for homesteading. Borah argued with Roosevelt and Gifford Pinchot over the need to withdraw so many acres of timber, coal, and phosphate from exploitation, but the argument concerned the amount, not the philosophy of conservation.

Borah's real impact was on national politics and policies that benefitted Idaho directly. He was in the forefront of many progressive struggles that resulted in needed reforms. During his first term in the Senate (1907–1913), Borah was heavily involved in three legislative battles that ultimately evolved into constitutional amendments. Knowing the desires of his constituents, Borah fought ably for the graduated income tax, the direct election of senators, and national Prohibition. Ironically, Borah opposed a constitutional amendment that would extend the right to vote to all women. Borah believed in woman suffrage, but he believed that it was a state's perogative to determine who could vote. Many people were terribly upset by Borah's reluctance to support a national suffrage amendment, and some even suggested that as the people's representative, he had no legal or moral right to set his individual views against the collective views of the people. His response was that he did "and then the people have the greater right to retire me." [1]

The people of Idaho never retired their famous senator. In 1912, he was re-elected even after Theodore Roosevelt had split the Republican party. During World War I, he won with Republican, Nonpartisan League, and Woodrow Wilson's support. When he sought a fourth term in 1924, the Republican party

1. Claudius Johnson, *Borah of Idaho* (Seattle: University of Washington Press, 1967), p. 84.

was again split with Borah's old Senate neighbor Robert LaFollette leading a Progressive faction into the wilderness, but Borah won easily. Borah was not affected by the depression-caused Democratic landslide of 1930, and he was able to withstand the combined challenge of C. Ben Ross and the New Deal in 1936. Every summer Borah would return to Idaho, rent a car, and drive around to visit the people. His oratorical gifts enabled him to speak to the loggers and farmers of Idaho as well as the leaders of the nation and be understood by both. Indeed, it was his ability as an orator that enabled Borah to receive wide acclaim throughout the nation.

Except for a brief flirtation with presidential primaries in 1936, Borah was content to use the Senate floor as the stage for his utterances on national and international affairs. He spurned two presidents when they sought his feelings on being appointed to the Supreme Court, and he rejected a potential offer to become secretary of state. His destiny was not served in committee meetings or on a judicial bench or in diplomatic negotiations or in high party circles. William Borah believed that his national contribution was as a spokesman against international involvement and as a vigilant watchdog for all the people.

Walter Lippmann tried to summarize Borah's philosophy in a 1936 essay. The editorialist called Borah "an individualist who opposed all concentration of power, who is against private privilege and private monopoly, against political bureaucracy and centralized government." [2] Borah never wavered on his commitment concerning monopoly and special privilege. Viewing the trusts and monopolies as outlaws that should be exterminated, Borah called the progressive battle to curb special interests just as important as the conflict between slavery and freedom. Borah was also morally indignant over the growing government bureaucracy and the evils of centralized power. Demanding economy and thrift, Borah constantly warned against undue spending extravagance on the part of the federal government shortly before the crash of 1929.

Once the depression hit, Borah's concept of federal spending

2. *New York Herald Tribune,* April 13, 1936.

changed drastically, and this new attitude of Borah's led to strained relations between the Idaho senator and Herbert Hoover, the new president. It is a fact that Borah and Hoover never hit it off well. Although Borah campaigned in Hoover's behalf, and Hoover approached him about becoming the secretary of state, they fought openly over what Borah considered Hoover's lack of appreciation for the plight of the destitute following the crash. Hoover hoped the states, cities, and charities could relieve the unemployed and poverty-stricken, but this orthodox approach to relief proved totally inadequate. Borah, keenly aware of Idaho's situation, wanted direct individual relief and fought for such legislation. When the administration successfully thwarted the proposal, an angry Borah told the Senate that he was ready to keep Congress in session "until the hungry are fed, until the sick are taken care of, until the Government of the United States has met its obligation to its diseased and hungry citizens." [3] Borah never relented in his attempts to obtain direct relief and at the same time expand the currency and get purchasing power to the people. He opposed Idaho's depression sales tax because it was a tax that was not based on the ability to pay. Prohibition was another issue which caused enmity between Borah and Hoover. Borah, an avowed dry, felt that Hoover was lax in enforcement procedures. Borah could work with Hoover on some matters, and although he differed with the president on tariff policies, farm relief, unemployment relief, governmental expenditures, and other issues, he was with Hoover on disarmament, treaties, and a reversal of the Latin American policy from dollar diplomacy toward the "good neighbor" policy. Borah's relations with Hoover's successor, Franklin Roosevelt, were similar.

Borah straddled the fence on many New Deal programs and ideas, but he did not intentionally harass Roosevelt. On some key issues, such as the recognition of Russia, Borah fought for the Roosevelt recommendation, but he also voted against such New Deal proposals as the court-packing scheme. However,

3. U.S. Senate, *Congressional Record,* Seventy-second Congress, 1st session, Feb. 2, 1931, p. 3760.

Borah supported Roosevelt's Supreme Court nominees, Hugo Black, Felix Frankfurter, and William Douglas. In fact, Borah was instrumental in getting the appointment offered to Douglas. His votes and behavior were determined by specific individuals and issues, and Borah was only consistent in his belief that he espoused a position of moral integrity. With Idaho's needs in mind, each New Deal measure was an individual entity that Borah worked for or against on its merits as he viewed them. He supported the Tennessee Valley Authority project, the Social Security Act, the Labor Relations Act, and public work projects. Borah opposed the National Recovery Act and the reciprocal tariff plan. He also voted against the Agricultural Adjustment Act because it did not guarantee the farmer the cost of production. On seventeen key New Deal measures, Borah voted with Roosevelt eleven times. Borah openly encouraged his own party to move in the direction of a more liberal stance. To him, a liberal was a person friendly to new ideas and one in favor of reform in the administration of government. In lay terms, Borah wanted to protect the rights of every American from the special interests and monopoly. That is why he found much of the New Deal congenial to his philosophy. Yet, it was in the area of foreign policy that Borah's moral vigilance led to much of his notoriety.

William Borah's battle with Woodrow Wilson over the League of Nations is well known and significant. The Idaho senator's conviction that the United States should remain totally aloof from international intrigue and alliances prompted him to lead the fight against the Treaty of Versailles. This moralistic commitment guided Borah in his opposition to the Treaty of Berlin, the Four-Power Treaty of 1922, and the World Court. However, as chairman of the Senate Foreign Relations Committee, Borah joined many liberals and idealists in pushing the Kellogg-Briand Pact, which supposedly outlawed war. The events of the 1930s shattered Borah's concept of a new world order, and the pact proved to be a bitter failure. By the late 1920s, Borah was convinced that relations with Latin America needed improvement, and he protested against American intervention throughout Central America and the Caribbean. Perhaps none of the above issues, however, is as significant as Borah's decade-long fight to recognize the Soviet Union.

Borah began advocating Soviet recognition as early as 1922, and he based his position on history and reality. He believed in the precedent set by the Founding Fathers of recognizing de facto governments, and he also believed that Soviet totalitarianism was better than the Czarist monarchy. The Idaho senator argued that trade with the Soviet Union would aid the economy and that the new Russian government could be trusted. Borah was also worried about the future peace in Europe and throughout the world. Borah argued that if the United States did not recognize a nation and had no diplomatic intercourse with it, the U. S. could not influence that nation in any way. In this instance, Borah was an avowed realist. Soviet propaganda could be handled, but the nation and government did exist, so when recognition came in 1933, Borah considered it a notable and worthwhile victory.

Borah represented Idaho and the nation well for more than three decades. He loved to speak and some argue that his career was dedicated to the effort to hear his own voice. Carefully cultivating reporters, Borah usually fared well in the nation's press. He sought, and obtained, a fantastic amount of publicity for a small western state. Yet, he shunned the opportunities for executive participation. Disliking routine and committee work, Borah was not the most able or willing Senate workhorse. His work during the 1920s as chairman of the Senate Foreign Relations Committee was notable, but not spectacular. Much of his time was spent preparing a speech to support or attack a current issue, not in guiding it through the channels leading to enactment. As with most educable people, Borah was inconsistent, and his views changed with the passing of time. His main consistency and his national legacy were that he had a moral commitment to create better opportunities for all Americans and that the United States had a commitment to create a better world in which to live.

Frank Church, a native of Boise, has also made an impact in the area of foreign policy as a senator. Appointed to the Foreign Relations Committee, he has been intimately involved with American foreign policy decisions. At one time he was a member of the U. S. delegation to the United Nations and his involvement has prompted the same charge from opponents that was leveled against Borah—that he is more interested in the world than in Idaho. Church, a fairly tall, good-looking man is much like Borah in many respects. A former college debater and American Legion orator, Church is an excellent speaker and performer. Although he was graduated from Stanford and attended Harvard, Church knows how to communicate with the common people in Idaho. Like Borah, Church married the daughter of a former governor. Bethine Church, daughter of Chase Clark, is a political asset to the senator and is well respected for her political "savvy" and approachable manner. Church is also a lawyer, but because he was elected to the Senate at age thirty-two, he has spent most of his professional career in legislative halls and not in courtrooms. Church has gone beyond Borah in the area of conservation; however, the pioneering work of Borah was necessary before the citizenry could be educated and could appreciate the genuine ecological crisis.

Church has won four elections in Idaho and has at times been the only Democrat to hold high office among the top leadership. He easily defeated the incumbent Herman Welker in 1956 even though the state voted for Eisenhower by an overwhelming margin. His closest election was in 1962, and then he overcame untraconservative challenges in 1968 and 1974. Church's career documents the contention that national political trends are often meaningless in Idaho. Most of Idaho's internal critics have forgotten that fact. In 1967, a recall Church movement was started in northern Idaho. Financed by California right-wing money, the initiators of the petition wanted Church ousted because he opposed the Vietnam War and was obstructing its prosecution. The Church-haters could not get the required 10 percent of the voters to sign the petition, and the next year Church was easily re-elected by the populace, in part because the recall plan backfired.

Church first vaulted into national headlines when he was chosen to keynote the 1960 Democratic convention in Los Angeles. From that point on, his activities have received national publicity. In his nearly twenty years as a senator, Church has supported many liberal and progressive measures. He voted for the legislation that resulted from the civil rights revolution of the 1960s. As a supporter of the civil rights acts of 1964 and 1965, Church also spoke out frequently against racial violence, the poll tax, and lynching. He has consistently voted for federal aid to education. Appointed as chairman of a special Committee on Aging, Church became keenly aware of the difficult problems facing elderly citizens of the nation. This committee launched investigations of Medicare (which Church supported), nursing homes, and other areas. In fact, probably one of the biggest differences between Church and Borah is that Church seemingly works harder in his committee assignments. Perhaps that is why Church was given the ticklish job of chairing the Special Committee on Intelligence. Investigating the abuses and operations of the Central Intelligence Agency and the Federal Bureau of Investigation was a direct result of the Watergate fiasco. In being chosen to chair this sensitive probe, Church obviously had a reputation for integrity, ability, and perspective.

Church's expertise and attention has mostly been directed toward two areas of great concern to the nation and Idaho, foreign policy and conservation. The diplomatic, military, and national trauma caused by the Vietnam War thrust Church into national prominence again. His positions have often been unpopular when taken, but historically he has fared well. This is especially true regarding the Vietnam War and his opposition to the conflict.

Senator Church began to oppose the escalation of the war early in the 1960s. He questioned the wisdom of Americanizing the war, bombing the north, and supporting Diem and successive military dictatorships. During the election year of 1964, Church had openly criticized the war to the point that he was classified in the national press as one of the Senate "doves." As more and more Americans were killed, Church's criticism intensified, and it ultimately led to an open split with Lyndon Johnson, even though they were both Democrats. As a member of the Foreign Relations Committee, Church listened to hours of testimony by government officials and concluded that the entire concept of American foreign policy cried for reassessment. American intrusions in the Dominican Republic, Laos, and Cambodia haunted Church as well as the quagmire that was Vietnam. William Borah would have been proud of his youthful successor.

Finally, frustrated by the decade-long war, Church joined other senators in trying to legislate a withdrawal. It was Church's constant contention that an indigenous war, a civil war, is the least susceptible to control by outsiders. In his opinion, the Americanization of the war only put the North Vietnamese in a better light in South Vietnamese eyes.

The internal divisiveness caused by the war upset Church. As campus protests turned into riots and bombings, the erosion of confidence was documented. Domestic destruction and death was an unwanted by-product of a foreign policy that went against the ideals expressed in the Declaration of Independence and the Bill of Rights.

Church's other great overriding senatorial concern has been directly related to Idaho's rivers, wildlife, trees, and mountains. To avid ecologists and dedicated conservationists, Senator Church has at times been found wanting. To committed proponents of mining, logging, and private power he is always an obstructionist. As a moderate, Church has often found himself in the middle of vicious disputes between the economically motivated exploiters and the nature-conscious preservationists. Although more pleasing to conservationists, Church has been criticized for stopping short and not going the full way with the ecologists. In part, Church's positions are tempered by the realization that he is often at odds with his congressional colleagues. Although Church has worked well with Republican Senators Dworshak, Jordan, and McClure, their concept of Idaho's needs and opportunities often differed greatly from Church's, which fact, once again, points to the inconsistency of Idaho's voters.

Church took office the year after the Eisenhower Administration capitulated and allowed the construction of three private power dams on the middle Snake River in Hells Canyon. Realizing the great hydroelectric potential of the lower Hells Canyon, power companies and the Army Corps of Engineers have been unceasing in their demand for more dams. At one point, in 1964, the Federal Power Commission approved the construction of another dam, but the Interior Department took the FPC to court, and the Supreme Court, in a landmark decision, struck down the FPC approval. Justice William Douglas, in writing the majority opinion, held that "a river is more than an amenity; it is a treasure." [4] The power companies persistently sought new approval for the dams—Mountain Sheep and Pleasant Valley. In the meantime, environmentalists were trying to get the middle Snake declared part of the National Wild and Scenic Rivers System. Idaho's new Democratic governor, Cecil Andrus, joined his Oregon and Washington counterparts in pushing for preservation of "a truly unique and magnificent treasure." Church was in the middle of a new Hells Canyon fight. Although he was firmly anti-dam, Church worked with Jordan and recommended a moratorium on dam building until 1978. The developmental interests were angry, but eventually the middle Snake River, with Church's support, became one of the recognized and preserved wild rivers.

Frank Church believes that the Wilderness Act was one of the most significant pieces of legislation for which he has worked. His support of it gained him the animosity of mining, timber, and grazing interests, and in the election of 1962 many Idahoans were upset with him. In spite of the organized opposition against him, Church won and learned a great political and humane lesson. He discovered that

> Idaho people cared a great deal about the outdoors. From that point on, men in public life in Idaho began to recognize that times were changing, that the long dominant interests in Idaho politics could no longer . . . preserve their rights to the public domain as against the public interest.[5]

As a cosponsor of the wild rivers concept, Church found that even a state so dependent on irrigated agriculture as Idaho was

---

4. Neal R. Peirce, *The Mountain States of America* (New York: W. W. Norton and Co., 1972), p. 147.

5. Peirce, *Mountain States*, p. 149.

learning that a river was "more than a potential irrigation ditch."

Church has discovered in Idaho's conservation battles that the federal bureaucracies are often as entrenched as the special interests. The U. S. Forest Service, Bureau of Reclamation, and Army Corps of Engineers are active lobbyists for their own proposals. Forest service philosophy is that timber is a crop; the Bureau of Reclamation needs dams in order to reclaim; the Corps of Engineers just wants to build. In order to steer wilderness, national park, or wild river systems through Congress, the federal bureaucracies are almost as great a problem as the special interest lobbyists. When Church sponsored legislation to create a Sawtooth National Park–National Recreation Area, the Forest Service joined mining, hunting, and timber interests in successfully postponing the measure. The idea of a simple national recreation area is repugnant to conservationists because it would still allow mining and other resource exploitation as well as intrusion by motorized vehicles. If the National Park Service administered the area, which, as proposed, included not only the Sawtooth and White Cloud ranges, but the Pioneer, Boulder, and Smoky mountains, the area would be closed to timber and mineral interests as well as hunters. Church upset the environmentalists again when he agreed to a 1971 compromise which created the Sawtooth National Recreation Area, temporarily banned mining, set aside some wilderness area, and directed the Interior Department to provide a Sawtooth National Park plan. Church worked to strengthen the bill, but some prospecting, subdividing, and cutting continued.

The great Idaho issue which crystallized opinion over conservation was the late 1960s proposal by the American Smelting and Refining Company that they open a 740-acre, open-pit mine to extract molybdenum from the magnificent White Cloud Range. The entire ecology of the mountains of central Idaho was endangered by the insensitive request to create a huge tailing pond for the open-pit project. By 1970, Church was joining Gov. Cecil Andrus and conservationists in a pitched battle to close completely the area to the mining interests. They saved the White Clouds by creating the Sawtooth National Recreation

Area, but their goal of giving the area national park status remained unfulfilled.

The mood and temper of the nation continually changes; yet Idaho's voters remain steadfast in their commitment to personalities as the main determination of political success or failure. Bethine Church described Idaho's voters along this vein. "If the people here trust you, they'll vote for you, even if they don't agree with you down the line. This is the essential thing about Idaho politics." [6] William Borah and Frank Church earned that trust and brought attention and admiration to the state that elected them. After a shaky and confused political beginning, Idaho has become a contributing part of the nation's political heritage.

6. Quoted in *Parade Magazine*, November 16, 1975, p. 5.

9

Idaho: A Beacon for the Future

In deciding whether to dam, mine, log, or otherwise develop the resources of the Snake River region, it is my own conviction that all of us will be more likely to make the right decisions if we approach them with "distance in our eyes" and place the rightful claims of the unborn alongside our own.

Stewart L. Udall, 1972

$\mathcal{O}$NE HUNDRED and seventy years after whites first discovered the area that became Idaho, the state still evokes an intriguing excitement. Beautiful and miraculously preserved, Idaho is one of the last bastions of a natural wonderland. It is virtually impossible to describe the breathtaking experience of standing on a peak in the Sawtooths, White Clouds, Seven Devils, Tetons, Big Horn Crags, Lost Rivers, or Clearwaters. The effect on the human intruder of the cold clean air, the open azure sky, and the green-carpeted mountains below is overcoming, and a powerful euphoria almost sweeps one from the high and lofty perches. It is just as overwhelming to lie prone upon a small windy mountain trail and sip at the icy clear water trickling from a spring and realize that within a few miles the water that seeps from the hillside will be cascading creek, then a raging river, that finally will reach the Pacific Ocean. Another emotional experience is to walk quietly upon needle carpet through the majestic white pine forests of northern Idaho and recall that some of these towering pines stood when Lewis and Clark, David Thompson, and Alexander Ross passed by.

This great natural legacy stands as a beacon to the nation. The observant native, however, is fully aware that there was a time when it was possible to stand on a knoll west of Idaho Falls and gaze at the towering Tetons on the eastern horizon— but now the phosphate plants, sawmills, and exhaust emissions create a continual haze that hovers over the Snake River valley. Magic valley residents are no longer guaranteed a view of central Idaho's sea of mountains to the north. The mining and logging operations of the Panhandle have similarly obstructed contemporary enjoyment of the rich beauty of that region. Or the August traveler who comes to see the Shoshone or Twin Falls may find a mere trickle of water slipping over the rocky precipice because almost the entire upstream river has been diverted for human needs. Twentieth-century technology is now a part of Idaho and its effects are omnipresent.

Idaho's history has been a continual saga of man either pitted against or exploiting the natural environment and the vast resources of the state. For much of its early existence, Idaho survived the human imprint. Native Americans never extracted a surplus, and they did not use the resources to accumulate wealth. Their existence depended on a continual replenishment of the earth. The activities of fur-trappers were ecologically disastrous, and their attitudes toward the beaver typifies much of the Idaho experience. In the rush to exterminate the resource, an insane competitiveness ruled. The gold and silver seekers gave no thought to the fact that they could not replenish the objects of their search. The early lumbermen operated with an exploitive mentality, and it was not until recent times that they were forced to adapt techniques to conserve and replenish the forests. At first, the tillers of the soil cared only about diverting life-giving water for their own individual or small group purposes. Little thought was given to what might happen to a dry downstream river bed. Only massive co-operation prevented a farmers' war and the total destruction of the Snake River system. For years, the local politicians have had to deal with the issues of Idaho's natural environment, and again, a partial commitment to preservation has only recently arisen. This history is part of the main-stream of the American experience, and only Idaho's relative isolation has helped to preserve it.

Census statistics indicate that Idaho's population reflects the mobility of the American people. Slightly over one-half of its residents were born in the Gem State. Because of proximity, Idaho exports people to its contingent neighbors at a high rate, but the state imports more from those states than are attracted away. More than thirty-two thousand residents of Utah were born in Idaho, but forty-four thousand Idahoans trace their birth-place to Utah. It is true that many Idahoans departed for the promised land of California at various times, but now approximately 10 percent of Idaho's people were born in California. Idaho's lower taxes, more space, and beautiful scenery made it an attractive oasis for tired urbanites.

Idaho also became a gathering area for one special immigrant group, the Spanish Basques. Their initial Idaho occupation was as herdsmen. Special immigration laws were passed that allowed Basque herders to be admitted in order to maintain a needed labor supply, but as soon as it was possible, they purchased land of their own or entered other occupations. Today, conscious of their heritage, second- and third-generation Idaho Basques have maintained a folk culture which is exhibited at their highly popular annual festival.

One community example of the problem between developer and preservationist is the current phenomenon of Boise, the state's capital city. Possessing a fine physical setting on the wooded Boise River, this comparatively small city of approximately one hundred thousand inhabitants is a strange amalgamation of all that is Idaho. Besides being located in a rich agricultural belt and being the state capital, Boise possesses other unique features. It is the corporate headquarters for many huge international conglomerates and has attempted to solve the problems of a developing urban center. Starting with the classic Mediterranean-style Union Pacific Depot, going north down Capital Boulevard past Boise State University, two large parks, and across the river to the Capitol, the observer will surely note that the city exudes prosperity and achievement. The stately older homes along the tree-sculptured boulevards of Harrison and Warm Springs add to the established sense of economic well-being.

The inner city reflects a newness that includes a Capital Mall, which encompasses the state offices and agencies. With the completion of headquarter buildings for the Bank of Idaho, Boise Cascade, and Morrison-Knudsen, the cityscape of Boise has gone perpendicular. The previously held contention that Boise was a center of repressive right-wing political activities is also changing. Although quite conservative, the community has evolved away from early abhorrence of any federal aid toward acceptance of such programs as slum clearance, housing codes, or environmental protection. Ironically, the proponents of urban renewal and the preservationists are constantly locking horns over the fate and value of Boise's earliest downtown buildings.

Like most Americans eternally wedded to the automobile, Boiseans take pride in the fact that from the time they leave home, they can be skiing at Bogus Basin in less than an hour, be elk or deer hunting in two hours, be at McCall in two hours and famous Sun Valley in three hours, or be duck hunting in forty-five minutes. The mountains and streams of Idaho beckon; yet, simultaneously, the economic motivation complicates the appreciation of nature's resources. Condominiums and other components of America's leisure civilization are victimizing the natural landscape.

Some decry the changes that come with time. The contrasting view of the evolution of Idaho's most noted resort, Sun Valley, is an example: According to old-time vacationers, the ornate beauty of Sun Valley that distinguished its existence from the 1930s until the late 1960s has been replaced by a mammoth resort that contrasts with rather than complements the little valley. With hundreds of condominiums at Sun Valley, or at Elkhorn of Sun Valley, a new development—that from a distance looks like a brightly colored Fisher-Price toy castle—and a new multistory Holiday Inn, Sun Valley is no longer unique nor especially attractive. It has become a haven for the wealthy, and its isolated atmosphere of fantasy is no more. The ski mountain is still there, but the vast expansion, apparently inevitable, has left a nostalgic tear in the eye of those who remembered an earlier day. However, attractiveness is in the eye of the beholder. A native Idahoan used to open spaces and no congestion might be appalled by a condominium development, but to an urbanite from Los Angeles, New York, or Chicago, Sun Valley still represents a blue-skied, sparsely inhabited paradise. McCall, a small town two hours north of Boise located on Payette Lake, is another example of leisure growth and expansion. The entire development of the Panhandle lakeside real estate illustrates the fact that growing private ownership makes public access limited. Those that are wealthy enough to maintain a second home or condominium have purchased their summer dream home at Hayden, Coeur d'Alene, or Pend Oreille. Consequently, Idahoans, in spite of their pride in their fantastic natural surroundings, have capitulated to the lure of the dollar and enticed outside money and people to develop a new brand of "stay-awhile and invest" tourism.

Idaho's beautiful natural setting has contributed in great measure to the corporate growth of Boise, and is one of the reasons many companies have not moved their headquarters to San Francisco, New York, or Chicago. Idaho, according to one executive, is a great place to live and rear a family. Boise Cascade is a good example of an Idaho-based company that remains in its original location. Under the leadership of Minnesota-born and Harvard-educated Robert V. Hansberger, Boise Cascade has become one of the one hundred largest corporations in the United States. Originally extracting a modest income from Idaho's forests, the firm diversified and began buying a number of firms in allied fields. Moving strictly from lumber to pulp, plywood, newsprint, boxes and office supplies, the Boise Cascade executives were not content. Residential homes, recreation lands, lakes, ski resorts, and urban development drew their attention. When a construction and real estate recession hit in the early 1970s, Boise Cascade found itself on the loss side of the ledger, but subsequently it regrouped and regained its solid footing.

Boise Cascade's environmental image, which is so important to the residents of Idaho, has been tarnished for quite some time. The land recreation boom of the late 1960s enticed the Boise firm into building a number of ski and hotel resort complexes in areas as widely separated as California and Vermont. Once the bulldozers and ready-mix cement trucks moved into previously forested areas, the conservationists were on the attack. The company pulled back again and was forced to restore the environment to its original beauty. Lately, the efforts of the company to obtain Forest Service permission to log the yellow pine of the Chamberlain Basin in the Idaho Primitive Area has caused another vicious battle between conservationists, the government, and the company.

The wealth of Boise Cascade still relies in part on the resources of Idaho's forests. Boise's agribusiness companies are similar. Both Ore-Idaho and J. R. Simplot are now Boise firms with millions of dollars of wealth based on potatoes and their by-products. Their success, like that of the large lumber company, is as dependent upon co-operation with the federal government as it is upon the irrigated acres of Idaho farmland. Simplot, a native of Iowa, moved to Idaho as a boy and soon made potato processing a successful enterprise. Always a step ahead of trends, Simplot moved into the dried vegetable business during World War II, and became the largest potato supplier to the armed forces. When there was a shortage of shipping boxes, he bought sawmills in order to guarantee his supply. Not content with potatoes, onions, and other vegetables, Simplot moved into the phosphate fertilizer business with a government loan to build a plant near Pocatello. Since suppliers were reluctant to provide him with ore, he acquired leases on government and Indian land east of Pocatello, and his company began mining phosphate ore. According to environmentalists, Simplot shows little concern for the ecological effects of open-pit mining or polluting Pocatello, and he just keeps pushing on. By the end of World War II, his scientists were experimenting with frozen potatoes. They finally made a breakthrough that provides Simplot one hundred million dollars in annual sales from his six processing plants, stretching from Idaho and Canada to Maine. Simplot's Idaho feedlots are capable of fattening one hundred fifty thousand steers and fifty thousand sheep annually, and his main feed ingredient is offal, the potato waste. The company has also been involved in residential development in Boise. Simplot, the farm boy who maintains a "down-home" frontier attitude, epitomizes the complexities that face Idaho. Exploit Idaho, grow upon it, develop it, enjoy its beauties—somehow everything will work out!

Boise is also the home of the mammoth Morrison-Knudsen Construction Company, one of the largest in the world. M-K, as it is called in Idaho, is involved in a variety of internationally significant projects from Asia to South America. In Idaho, much of their work has dealt with dam and road construction, as well as mining. Internationally, M-K was heavily involved in Vietnam with numerous military contracts and the company has received the bid for many projects in Latin America. It was also a major contractor for the subway tunnels under San Francisco Bay. Typifying the stable wealth of Boise, the M-K owners have contributed to the development of the arts, a large city park, and other philanthropic endeavors.

Albertson's, a large western retail grocery chain, is also headquartered at the mother store in Boise. By the early 1970s, it ranked in the top fifty of American retail outlets and was invading the rapidly expanding markets of Texas and the Southwest. An interesting feature of Albertson's, Morrison-Knudsen, and Simplot is that they all started out as small family enterprises and their growth parallels the development of Boise and the entire state.

Although much of Boise's development is attributed to the economic success of its corporate inhabitants, more is probably caused by the growth of state government and the service-related industries. Many Boise natives are desirous of seeing the new Boise State University surpass its two sister universities as Idaho's mecca of learning. It seems apparent that Boise's rise to a Rocky Mountain and western corporate headquarters will further accentuate the "discovery" of Idaho and the demands on its resources. This is especially true of Idaho's desirable and seemingly inexhaustible supply of water.

If there is one thing that Idahoans are selfish about, it is their water. All that is needed to incite violent arguments is to suggest that Idaho water might be diverted to Nevada, California, or the Southwest through the tributaries of the Colorado River or by gigantic pipelines. Once again, as in the past, Idahoans face present and future conflicts over the streams that provide more than seventy million acre-feet annually. That is nearly five times as much as the Colorado River system, which is the supplier for much of the American Southwest. Many Idahoans feel that more Idaho desert remains to be reclaimed and ask why Gem State water should provide life to arid lands in Nevada and California. In addition, a shift in some Idahoans' thinking has made it difficult for the federal and local proponents of reclamation and hydroelectric power to further dam the Snake and its tributaries. Many activists feel that there are enough dams, canals, and power plants.

Idaho is currently engulfed in a vigorous conservationist movement. It is in the area of wildlife, wilderness management, and water utilization that Idaho's devotees disagree. When the huge Mountain Home Reclamation Project was proposed in the late 1960s, one aspect of opposition used by conservationists was that the proposed project would do considerable damage to fish, wildlife, and, especially, golden eagles and prairie falcons, whose Idaho nesting concentrations are the greatest in the United States. Mountain sheep, elk, moose, and steelheads—all are of concern to the dedicated environmentalist. Every proposed irrigation or hydroelectric project will undergo scrutiny closer than ever before, and pork-barrel projects designed to bring prosperity to a locale rather than to provide an absolutely necessary dam may be a thing of the past. Rabid conservationists claim that the last two major projects of the Snake River system, the Dworshak on the North Fork of the Clearwater River, and the Teton on the Teton River, were both based on pork-barrel politics and not agricultural or power needs. In fact, the ill-fated Teton Dam broke on June 5, 1976, and flooded the entire valley. Of course, other interest groups disagree vehemently, and thus the debate continues. But Idaho's experience indicates that in this small, remote state, the battle among governmental bureaucracies, corporate interests, and environmentalists will be fought on more even terms than earlier had seemed possible. This development in the relationship of the people to the nature which provides them life's necessities is of far-reaching importance.

In many respects Idaho is still a frontier, but one which decries the invasion of its privacy. Contemporary Idaho's most significant role in the future might be that of an example to the rest of the United States as to how growth, exploitation, and utilization may be held in check. Perhaps the most important national conservation battles in the last third of the twentieth century will be fought over the Idaho wilderness. Every American has a vested interest in the outcome of these confrontations. The grave national questions of resource use, population growth, food production, industrialization, and energy consumption can, in part, be answered in the mountains, streams, lakes, and people of Idaho. Indeed, the answers may come from the ancient philosophy of those native Americans who held an almost religious conviction that the land, water, and air were sacred components of a divine nature.

This is the road Idaho history has pursued. Remote and isolated, it has never been victimized by the mainstream onslaughts of civilization. The rugged desert and mountain terrain made settlement, transportation, and communication most difficult. After nearly two centuries of recorded history, it is clear that Idaho retains some simple individualistic political characteristics and some complex co-operative economic tendencies. A politician with strong personal appeal who demonstrates honesty may succeed, but without federal and eastern capital, transportation, reclamation, and mining development would have been severely retarded. Without the promptings of federal administrations and, especially, the New Deal, a conservation mentality might not have developed quickly enough to save parts of Idaho. Obviously—and this fact compounds the issues, since most of the Gem State is federally owned—there is still a great demand on the part of Idahoans for federal co-operation in the multiple use of the land. The degree of use is the crux of the controversy.

Idaho is one of only a few relatively unspoiled states left in the United States. Perhaps the most basic of questions is whether or not growth, development, industry, and change should be encouraged or discouraged. In an arid state with more than 70 percent public land, maybe eight people per square mile is enough. How the special-interest groups work with the federal and state politicians and how the people tolerate their collective behavior will determine whether Idaho is content with quality of life and is not tempted by quantity. Perhaps Idaho can have its natural beauty, prosper from it, and preserve it. Some think that an economy based on agriculture and controlled scenic tourism is the course Idaho should follow. Senators James McClure and Church lean in this direction and are increasingly aware of the need for balance in the utilization of resources.

Senator Church has said:

This corner of the country has always had the advantages of continental isolation. Its less crowded climes and its outdoor environment have provided a wholesome life which proves that monetary levels need not be the dominant ingredient in what we call "our standard of living." Indeed, Idaho might well claim the nation's highest standard of living, if measured by our pace of life, by our hospitable, crime-free neighborhoods, by our mountains and streams, and our many other escape hatches from 20th century pressures.[1]

Senator McClure adds:

The challenge we all face in Idaho is how we can maintain the proper balance between man and the natural environment we have while maintaining a sufficient base so our citizens can make a living and pay taxes to support education, social services and other governmental functions. This will not be an easy task but I am confident that the pioneer determination and ability of our citizens will meet the challenge and Idaho will continue to be the great state it is.[2]

Gov. Cecil Andrus is more cognizant of Idaho's ecology than any previous occupant of the statehouse. It is fortunate that the leaders Idaho needs for its future are politicians who care more

1. Sen. Frank Church to Ross Peterson, November 25, 1975, letter in author's possession.
2. Sen. James McClure to Ross Peterson, November 21, 1975, letter in author's possession.

about Idaho's priceless physical heritage than the prosperity that would accompany an open-pit mine.

The dream that Idaho inspires is one of preserving unspoiled wild country. That is the state's most distinctive resource. A nation or a state cannot afford to let its machines destroy its nature-bestowed gifts. To follow the pattern of enticing people to Idaho with amusement parks, luxury hotels, and motorized recreation would defeat the purpose and reality of Idaho. The beauty and peacefulness of the state could be undermined by the by-products of a leisure-oriented, consuming public. Perhaps it is a fond dream that Idaho may show the nation and society the way from its materialism toward the dawn of a new day when nature in its raw and rugged state will be a prize worthy of preservation. (But then, it may be that it is Idaho's air, trees, and water that inspire such peaceful aberrations of the mind.) Two hundred years ago, Thomas Paine, writing during the winter of 1776, described a crisis situation analogous to Idaho's current dilemma. In trying to strengthen the resolve of American patriots, Paine wrote that the success or failure of the experiment was "wholly owing to the constitution of the people and not to the constitution of the government." If the Idaho people's constitution is of the magnitude of its rivers, mountains, wild flowers, and game, these people will bequeath their proud physical heritage to a subsequent generation, yet unborn.

Suggestions for Further Reading

Any study of Idaho now begins with the *History of Idaho,* 3 vols. (New York: Lewis Historical Publishing Co., 1959), by Merrill D. Beal and Merle W. Wells. Wells, longtime director of the Idaho Historical Society, and Beal, a retired Idaho State University historian, did an excellent job in developing the main themes of Idaho's history. The first two volumes are especially valuable as narrative history, and the third is a biographical addition featuring prominent Idahoans. Wells's *A Short History of Idaho* (Boise: Idaho Historical Society, 1974) and *Idaho: A Student's Guide to Localized History* (New York: Teacher's College, Columbia University Press, 1965) also demonstrate the writer's wide knowledge of the state. A volume edited by Richard W. Etulain and Bert W. Marley, *The Idaho Heritage: A Collection of Historical Essays* (Pocatello: Idaho State University Press, 1974) is an excellent addition to Idaho's general histories. The WPA-inspired and Vardis Fisher-edited *Idaho: A Guide in Word and Pictures* (Caldwell: Caxton Printers, 1937) and *The Idaho Encyclopedia* (Caldwell: Caxton Printers, 1938) still possess merit and are worthy sources. Undoubtedly the best and most complete Idaho bibliography compiled was done by Richard W. Etulain and Merwin Swanson, *Idaho History: A Bibliography* (Pocatello: Idaho State University Press, 1975). There are numerous local and regional histories of varied value, but Merrill D. Beal's *A History of Southeastern Idaho* (Caldwell: Caxton Printers, 1942) and Grace Jordan's *Home Below Hells Canyon* (Lincoln: University of Nebraska Press, 1954) are two of special note.

Although a number of exciting articles have appeared, especially in *Idaho Yesterdays,* monographs dealing exclusively with Idaho are still somewhat sparse. Those cited are among the best available, but they represent only a skeleton of the total picture.

The best anthropological studies of Idaho's native Americans are Deward E. Walker, Jr., *American Indians of Idaho* (Moscow: University of Idaho Press, 1971) and Sven Liljeblad, *Indian Peoples of Idaho*

(Pocatello: Idaho State College, 1957). Neither of these studies has received the circulation they deserve. Brigham Madsen, *The Bannock of Idaho* (Caldwell: Caxton Printers, 1958) is a fine book, and the author's anticipated histories of the Shoshonis and Lemhis will add significantly to the literature. On Chief Joseph and the Nez Percé War see Merrill D. Beal, *"I Will Fight No More Forever": Chief Joseph and the Nez Percé War* (Seattle: University of Washington Press, 1963) and Mark H. Brown, *The Flight of the Nez Percé* (New York: Putnam's Sons, 1967).

There are a number of fine studies of Idaho political history. Merle Wells's doctoral dissertation, which is soon to be published, "The Idaho Anti-Mormon Movement, 1872–1908" (University of California, 1950), is the definitive work on that controversial subject. Fred T. Dubois, the Mormon baiter, told his side, and it was published by Louis J. Clements, *Fred T. Dubois's The Making of a State* (Rexburg: Eastern Idaho Publishing Company, 1971). William E. Borah has attracted numerous scholars, but five volumes of significance have emerged from historians' research: Claudius O. Johnson, *Borah of Idaho* (Seattle: University of Washington Press, 1967); Darrell L. Ashby, *The Spearless Leader: Senator Borah and the Progressive Movement in the 1920's* (Urbana: University of Illinois Press, 1972); John C. Vinson, *William E. Borah and the Outlawry of War* (Athens: University of Georgia Press, 1957); Marian C. McKenna, *Borah* (Ann Arbor: University of Michigan, 1961); and Robert J. Maddox, *William E. Borah and American Foreign Policy* (Baton Rouge: Louisiana State University Press, 1969). Of these, only the Johnson book discusses much of Borah's career in Idaho and Idaho problems while Borah was in the Senate. One of the finest monographs on Idaho politics is Michael P. Malone, *C. Ben Ross and the New Deal in Idaho* (Seattle: University of Washington Press, 1970). When Ross Peterson's *Prophet Without Honor: Glen H. Taylor and the Fight for American Liberalism* (Lexington: University of Kentucky Press, 1974) is added to Malone it provides an example of what has been done. Many other political figures are worthy of such biographies.

The mining experience in Idaho is covered by John Fahey, *The Bullyhoo Bonanza: Charles Sweeny and the Idaho Mines* (Seattle: University of Washington Press, 1971); William S. Greever, *Bonanza West: The Story of the Western Mining Rushes* (Norman: University of

Oklahoma Press, 1963); and Rodman W. Paul, *Mining Frontiers of the Far West, 1848–1880* (New York: Holt, Rinehart, and Winston, 1963). Agriculture and water development history need further study, but a dissertation by W. Darrell Gertsch, "The Upper Snake River Project: A Historical Study of Reclamation and Regional Development, 1890–1930," University of Washington, 1974, is excellent. It is hoped that Gertsch will expand his study in order to cover post-depression development, and have it published. Leonard Arrington, *Beet Sugar in the West: A History of the Utah-Idaho Sugar Company, 1891–1966* (Seattle: University of Washington Press, 1966) and J. R. Bachman, *Story of the Amalgamated Sugar Company, 1897–1961* (Caldwell: Caxton Printers, 1962) demonstrate what can be done with agrarian-business history. The Simplots, Albertsons, and Boise Cascade need similar studies by professional historians. Glen Barrett's *J. Lynn Driscoll: Western Banker* (Boise: Syms-York, 1974) is a good study of twentieth-century banking.

There are a number of fine historians who are in the process of publishing on Idaho. Robert Sims, Glen Barrett, Hugh Lovin, Richard Etulain, and Bert Marley are only a few. Anything that they produce will be noteworthy and necessary. Sims's study of Japanese in Idaho will provide essential insights and Etulain's knowledge of Basques as well as his expertise in literary history offers a needed dimension. The final story of the fate of Idaho's natural environment is left to its people and the government, but Boyd Norton's *Snake River Wilderness* (San Francisco: Sierra Club, 1972) gives a pessimistic indication of the final outcome. Two excellent pictorial depictions of Idaho's varied environment are Bill Gulick, *Snake River Country* (Caldwell: Caxton Printers, 1971) and an Idaho National Bank-funded and Robert O. Beatty-written *Idaho* (Caldwell: Caxton Printers, 1975).

In the final analysis, Idaho's historiography corresponds to the natural situation within the state: both are in their adolescence and have much to offer historians and the nation.

Index

197

Hill, Joe, 114
Home Owners Loan Corporation, 150
Homestead Act, 94, 124, 128–129, 171
Horses, 22–24
Hoset, Father Joseph, 45
Howard, Gen. O. O., 76–83 *passim;* 86
Hudson's Bay Company, 32, 40, 41, 42, 46, 47
Humbird, John, 116
Humbird, Thomas, 120
Hunt, Wilson Price, 34–35
Hunter, Chief Bear, 73, 74

Idaho: origin of name, 3, 64; as crossroads, 4; boundaries of, 5–6, 13–14, 47, 65; as "pregnant capital L," 5, 18; as territory, 5, 32, 62–64, 68, 91–92; size of, 6; elevation of, 12; as three Idahos, 18. *See also* Statehood
Idaho and Oregon Land Improvement Company, 103
Idaho City, 58–59
Idaho Irrigation District Thirty-Six, 128, 134–135
Idaho Mining and Irrigation Company, 125–127
Idaho Nonpartisan League (INPL), 143–144, 165–166
Idaho Organic Act, 64
Idaho Power Company, 135, 136
Idaho Primitive Area, 8, 187
Idaho Reclamation Association, 134
Idaho Test Oath Act, 95–96
Income, 144–146, 158
Indians: harmony of with nature, 22; relations with Mormons, 50–52; fences incomprehensible to, 69; and Whitman massacre, 70; on reservations, 87–89; population of, 88, 89; suicide rate of, 88. *See also* Fort Hall, names of tribes
Industrial Workers of the World, 113, 152, 164. *See also* Labor
Irrigation. *See* Water

Jackson, Donald, 40
Jackson Lake, 133, 134, 135
Jacobs, Frank, 103
Jefferson, Thomas, 24, 30
Jewett, G. F. ("Fritz"), 121

Johnston, Albert Sidney, 51
Jones, Witcher, 130
Jordan, Len B., 159, 178, 179
Joseph, Chief, 21, 75–80 *passim*
Joseph, Old, 76

Kellogg, Noah, 105–106
Ketchum, David, 103
Killebrew, Harmon, 169
Kimberly, Peter, 130, 131
Kootenai Indians, 20, 89
Ku Klux Klan, 165
Kullyspell House, 11, 33, 34, 38

Labor: and unions in Coeur d'Alene mines, 108–110; unrest of in 1935 and 1936, 151–152; and logger's strike in 1917, 164–165; and "Wobblies," 165, 166. *See also* Industrial Workers of the World; Western Federation of Miners
Lakes, 10–12
Last Chance Mine, 106
Law, Vernon, 169
Lead mining, 104–114
Lee, Jason, 43
Lemhi Indians, 20, 74–75
Lemhi River, 25, 26, 27
Lewis and Clark expedition, 24–32
Lewiston: as supply headquarters, 56, 57; as seat of territorial government, 64, 65; replaced as capital, 66; mentioned, 60, 62, 63
Lisa, Manuel, 34
Longheme, Henry, 59
Lumber industry: and exploitation of timber, 15; production of, 16; Idaho as leading state in, 116; and Boise Cascade Corporation, 116, 119, 122, 185–188; and Potlatch Forests Incorporated (PFI), 116, 119, 120–122; and Payette Lumber and Manufacturing Company, 117, 121; and forest fires, 118–119, 147; and shipping costs, 119; and shipping via Panama, 119; and lack of quick profit, 119–120; and Clearwater Company, 120; and Boise Payette company, 121–122; ecological damage, 123; during depression, 145; recovery by 1939, 158; logger's strike in 1917,